How to plan a wedding without killing anyone

Katie Dundas-Todorov

All rights reserved.

No part of this publication may be reproduced in any form or by any electronic or mechanical means, including information storage or retrieval systems, without written permission from the author, except for the use of brief quotations.

Disclaimer: please note this book is intended as advice and guidance only, no responsibility is taken for choices you may make using this book.

Although the author has made every effort to ensure that the information in the book was correct at the time of publication, the author does not assume and hereby disclaims any liability to any party for loss, damage or disruption caused by errors, omissions or information that has changed since the date of publication.

Real-life events and experiences referred to throughout the book are detailed only from the author's point of view, and as such it should be recognised that this is not necessarily a complete and unbiased recollection.

"Sing like the birds sing, not worrying about who hears or what they think." ~Rumi

CONTENTS

Foreword i

Chapter One
You're Engaged! 1

Chapter Two
Task List Overview 10

Chapter Three
Wedding Spreadsheet 21

Chapter Four
The Budget 29

Chapter Five
The Location/venue(s) 40

Chapter Six
Wedding-planning-free Days 51

Chapter Seven
The Wedding/Bridal Party 58

Chapter Eight
The Wedding Website 70

Chapter Nine
The Guest List 78

Chapter Ten
Wedding Stationery 87

Chapter Eleven
Dealing With Difficult People 98

Chapter Twelve
The Bride's Outfit 110

Chapter Thirteen
Hair and Make-up 121

Chapter Fourteen
The Groom's Outfit 132

Chapter Fifteen
Bridal Party Outfits 140

Chapter Sixteen
The Hen and Stag Do 150

Chapter Seventeen
Photography and Videography 159

Chapter Eighteen
The Ceremony 175

Chapter Nineteen
Transport 185

Chapter Twenty
Decoration 194

Chapter Twenty-one
Flowers 204

Chapter Twenty-two
Music and Entertainment 216

Chapter Twenty-three
Food and Drink 226

Chapter Twenty-four
The Seating Plan 236

Chapter Twenty-five
Speeches 247

Chapter Twenty-six
The Cake 255

Chapter Twenty-seven
The Rehearsal Dinner 265

Chapter Twenty-eight
On the Day Organisation 274

Chapter Twenty-nine
Final Note 282
Acknowledgments... 284

Foreword

Just a few years ago, in March, my now husband proposed to me. Though we had spoken about and long known we intended to marry, his proposal was a wonderful surprise. We decided to marry later that year, in November, as we both loved the idea of a late autumn wedding and the timing worked well for us. This left us with less than eight months to plan our dream wedding!

When it came to wedding planning, neither of us had been to many weddings. This was a wonderful opportunity as it meant we didn't have many prior conceptions about what a wedding should be, so it meant we naturally made the day our own. However, it was also quite daunting at first, as we had no idea where to begin in many areas.

I read extensively, and many of the books seemed to assume a basic level of wedding planning knowledge, which we simply didn't have. This meant an awful lot of Googling, asking friends and relatives for advice and posting questions on Facebook groups as well as stepping on a few toes at times, completely unintentionally. It seemed strange that all of this information wasn't just available in one place, as it would have made the wedding planning process a lot easier and more enjoyable!

Having successfully planned our wedding together, I decided to compile all of this research into one book with the hope of making wedding planning a less complex and more pleasurable process for all who read it.

This book and all of its ideas and information have been developed alongside friends who have also recently married or are soon to be married (the last few years have been a popular period for weddings amongst our friendship groups). Throughout this book I emphasise the importance that your wedding is unique to you as a couple, so having so many points of view come together in one book is invaluable.

Please feel free to read the book from start to finish if you so wish or dive into specific sections you need a little more advice around. The book aims to serve both as an informative book and a guide to make your own wedding planner. Each chapter will end with a summary of its main points and a suggested page for your wedding planning folder. The wedding planner is of course entirely optional, but thoroughly recommended as it will help to keep all your ideas and plans in one place.

Though I frequently use the terms bride and groom throughout the book, I implore you to delete and replace the terms and chapters as required to make the book more relevant to you as a couple. Love is love, whether there are two brides, two grooms or whatever combination, and a wedding is a celebration of love. Never let anyone dull your sparkle, or, in the words of Taylor Swift, (to make this more wedding appropriate), "Like can you just not step on my gown?".

Chapter One

You're Engaged!

Congratulations – you're engaged! If not, I'm assuming you're super organised and already planning ahead. For the purposes of this book, I'm going to assume you're engaged. If this is the case then I beg of you, please read this first chapter then put away this book for at least a week and instead focus on celebrating, there's plenty of time for wedding planning later.

Proposals, like rings and even partners, come in all styles, shapes and sizes. What's important is that it is special to the both of you. I would suggest, even if you don't normally keep a diary, writing down a little something is a great idea for both of you. It can all seem a little surreal at the time, like a dream come true, so writing something down can help make it seem more real and help you to remember all the

How To Plan A Wedding Without Killing Anyone

little details forever. A rough outline of what you might like to include:

- When the proposal took place
- What you did that day – any fun activities
- Where you went
- Who you saw that day and who was involved in the proposal
- (If you were the one proposing), how you planned the proposal
- How you felt – perhaps the most special part, how did you feel the moment he or she proposed to you or that you proposed to them

Our Proposal Story

....
....
....
....
....
....
....
....
....
....
....
....
....

"The more you praise and celebrate your life, the more there is in life to celebrate!"

-Oprah Winfrey

How To Plan A Wedding Without Killing Anyone

During the wedding planning process, in times of stress especially, it can be nice to reread this and remind yourself of your engagement day. Furthermore, years from now, when it all seems a distant memory, this can help you remember that special moment. It doesn't need to be an essay but believe me, your future self will thank you!

Following the proposal is a time for happiness and celebration, you're getting married! Try not to think about plans and logistics. When people ask questions which you haven't even thought about the answer to, it's perfectly ok to simply explain to them "Oh, we're still celebrating our engagement, we haven't started to plan anything yet".

> ### Top Tip
>
> Make sure to take some time to celebrate just the two of you before getting on the phone to tell everyone. Even just take 30 minutes to cuddle; this is a time you will treasure forever!

Furthermore, try not to be panicked if or when someone asks you about something you had no idea was even a thing! The day after we got engaged, one relative asked me what theme we had chosen for the wedding; I had no idea how to answer this. At the time, I didn't even know weddings could have a theme! Not to worry, this book will guide you through all of this in an enjoyable and fun way, but for now, focus on celebrating!

You're Engaged!

I hear you asking, but how do I celebrate? Well, celebrate as you would any other big life event – doing whatever it is that you enjoy! Some ideas for celebrating your engagement include:

1. Pop the bubbly! Celebrate with your favourite fizz or drink – if there's a special drink that means something to the both of you then be original and go for that. Take some photos too – of all our engagement and wedding photos, for me perhaps the most special are the selfies my now husband and I took on the evening we got engaged. I hadn't done my nails (my only engagement regret!), my hair was a mess and I've no idea what my face was doing in most the photos – but it was an evening of pure bliss and I'm so happy we took these photos!

2. Go for a nice walk, perhaps even to a special place and take some engagement photos whilst that engagement excitement is still fresh. These, like photos from the proposal day, are ones you will treasure forever. Also, it's chance to take nice photos with your hair, make-up, outfit and most importantly nails planned if you so choose.

3. Revisit your first date – wherever it was, go back and have an amazing time. Laugh at the awkwardness of your first date, reminiscence over how you felt and celebrate how far you've come. Whether it was a bar,

a restaurant or something way more out there, this place will always be incredibly special to the both of you and that's definitely worth celebrating!

4. Recreate some of your favourite dates – my now husband and I once made pizza from scratch together and had an absolute whale of a time – so we did this again to celebrate a few days after we got engaged.

5. Take an engagement-cation – so I'm not sure this is actually a thing – but why not! This is an amazing time in your life so why not make it even more special with a spontaneous weekend away somewhere romantic. These days there are lots of websites and apps with last minute trips so seize the moment and jet off for a few days somewhere to celebrate. This has the added bonus of giving you time as a couple to focus on celebrating.

6. Let your friends and family know – be sure to do so before updating your social media! No loved one will be happy if they find out through Facebook that you're engaged so avoid that minefield!

7. Update your social media and of course profile pic – this is an exciting time to share with everyone and social media allows you to proudly shout out your good news from the rooftops. Ring selfies are a must – and you'll more than likely find your ring in the

foreground becomes your natural way of posing no matter how strange the pose you have to pull to make it so.

8. Traditionally the newly engaged woman can buy her husband-to-be a shiny new watch to celebrate their engagement. Moving things to the 21st century, it's nice to take this tradition and make it your own. A friend of mine whose girlfriend proposed to her decided it would be nice to propose back so that they both got their magical proposal moment and let me tell you it was an absolutely beautiful day and so incredibly special for both of them.

Following on from this, weddings are a celebration of love, more specifically your love as a couple. Many people say the most enjoyable weddings are those that take things that are special to and make the couple unique and celebrate them. So why not start now, celebrate in your own wonderful and unique style! Feel free to jot down some celebration ideas:

....
....
....
....
....
....
....
....
....

How To Plan A Wedding Without Killing Anyone

Summary

- Try to write even a brief note or diary entry about your proposal day – it's a memory you'll treasure forever!

- Focus on celebrating for now, there's plenty of time for wedding planning later!

- Take lots of photos!

- Don't panic when people ask questions you have no idea how to answer, politely tell them you are still celebrating and haven't started planning yet.

You're Engaged!

Wedding Planner

....

&

....

Chapter Two

Task List Overview

<u>Wedding planning folder</u>

First task: getting organised. In my experience there are two types of people when it comes to wedding planning. One: those who head straight out to the shops to buy a wedding planning organiser and two: those who just make notes on paper and leave it in a pile.

The former (I myself fell into this group) waste almost £20 on a planner they barely use. Don't get me wrong, the planner looked amazing and made me feel so organised when I admired it sitting pride of place on my coffee table. But there are numerous sections that we just didn't use – a section for our guest list

<u>Top Tip</u>
Don't bother buying an expensive wedding planner – make your own personalised one.

Task List Overview

with all their contact information, for example. This is the 21st century, I'm not writing all that out – I have it in a spreadsheet (further details in chapter nine). Instead I was left with the useless task of completing sections I simply didn't need, that or accepting numerous empty pages which I felt guilty for not having completed. Every time I looked through my beautiful book, the shame and embarrassment of the completely unnecessary but uncompleted tasks hung over me.

The latter with their piles upon piles of notes, mentioning no names here, are happy to begin with. However, as the pile of notes builds, chaos builds and the inevitable panic ensues when you need to find a specific sheet of paper with that specific piece of information.

Life usually teaches us that the optimum option is somewhere in the middle. This also rings true here. What I recommend is a beautiful A4 ring binder folder – pick a nice one out together – filled with transparent sleeves and, if you feel like it maybe even some snazzy dividers. The added bonus of transparent sleeves is that they provide

> **Top Tip**
>
> Join wedding groups on Facebook by searching for groups with the word "Wedding" in. These groups are full of amazing ideas, great value suppliers and generally juicy stories. Just be careful not to get too caught up in them, always check out suppliers before handing over money and pay via PayPal or credit card for added protection.

storage for any leaflets, flyers and cards you will inevitably pick up at wedding fairs.

Make your own wedding planning file personalised to your own needs and wants. Do feel free to have a sneaky look at the shop bought ones to get an idea of what you want to include or don't really need in your own file and go with that.

A few ideas for sections in your folder to include:

- A nice title page with your names on
- Task List
- Wedmin – details of your wedding email account, bank account and insurance
- The budget
- Venue ideas
- The Wedding Party
- Website ideas
- Guest list planning
- Save the Date ideas
- Invitations and other Stationery ideas
- Gift List
- Bride's outfit, hair and make-up
- Groom's outfit and grooming
- Photography and videography ideas
- Music ideas
- Entertainment ideas
- Decoration ideas
- Food and drink ideas

Task List Overview

- Flower ideas
- Cake ideas
- Transport ideas
- Hen ideas
- Stag ideas
- Ceremony ideas
- Seating plan
- Speeches
- On the day organisation documents
- Rehearsal dinner ideas
- Overall Suppliers list with payment dates and contact details
- Honeymoon plans

> **Top Tip**
>
> Join Pinterest - it's really easy to use and full of amazing ideas. Be aware you can get lost in it for hours flicking through ideas!

Please remember that many blank pages are to be expected for now – this book will help you fill them in as you read through. At the end of each chapter, an optional blank template for a page in your folder is provided. Pick and choose what works for you as a couple.

Wedding planning task list

There is no perfect amount of time in which to plan a wedding – some people take years, others months and some even just weeks. I hope you're beginning to notice a theme in this book – doing it your own way is perfectly ok.

"Focus on being productive instead of being busy"
-Tim Ferris

Task List Overview

A lot of wedding planning books will set out a twelve-month checklist – this left me, a bride with eight months to plan, quite concerned I might be attempting too much. Thankfully, as perhaps a level-headed person would have predicted, everything went perfectly and no-one turned up four months later expecting to be attending or supplying on that day.

Rather than a rigid month-by-month wedding organisation plan, because I don't know any of my friends who have stuck to one, I've decided it's better to provide a list of wedding tasks. These are in a rough order of what should be done earlier and what can be done later:

Ideally earlier:
- Decide budget
- Decide on the type of ceremony – religious or civil - and location
- Choose date and time of ceremony
- Book celebrant
- Research reception venues
- Make and send out save the dates
- Take out wedding insurance
- Draft guest list
- Decide on wedding party
- Book reception venue
- Create wedding spreadsheet
- Create a joint wedding email address

How To Plan A Wedding Without Killing Anyone

At some point between one year and one month before your wedding day you must both give notice of marriage at your local registry office. For this, you will need to have booked your venue already. If you are marrying in a Church of England church you must instead see your local vicar, who will arrange for Banns to be read and will then issue their own certificate allowing the marriage to take place.

Research each at your own pace and book or buy when it feels right:

- Caterers and menus
- Wedding dress
- Groom's outfit
- Dress and suit fittings
- Hair and makeup and trials
- Wedding stationary including invitations
- Photographer
- Videographer
- Wedding party outfits
- Wedding cake
- Florist
- Wedding transport
- Entertainment
- Music or DJ
- Wedding rings
- Honeymoon, visas and travel insurance

Again, decide and design these at your own pace, make them your own and enjoy the process:

Task List Overview

- Wedding website (if having one)
- Order of service
- Readers for ceremony
- Witnesses for ceremony
- Wedding gift list
- Decor
- Wedding day favours or gifts
- Readings
- Music
- Seating plan
- Photo list for photographer

Please note that for popular wedding dates (especially the summer) suppliers can book up for years in advance. Be aware that the sooner you research and book things the more likely the supplier is to be available for your date. I would therefore suggest starting with things that are a priority for you as a couple. For example, if there's a must-have florist you desperately want to supply your flowers, start here and book them while they are still available.

About a month before your wedding day:
- Send out confirmation email to all suppliers for peace of mind
- Write a rough plan of the actual day's timings

How To Plan A Wedding Without Killing Anyone

Summary

- Design your own wedding planning folder using the planner pages found at the end of each chapter as a template.

- There is not perfect amount of time in which to plan a wedding, find what works for you.

- There isn't a specific order to complete tasks and, contrary to many wedding planning timelines, there are few actual hard deadlines when it comes to wedding planning.

- Do remember that suppliers can book up, so try to book earlier to avoid disappointment with unavailability if you are hankering after a specific supplier.

Task List

- Decide budget
- Decide on the type of ceremony - religious or civil - and location
- Choose date and time of ceremony
- Book celebrant
- Research reception venues
- Make and send out save the dates
- Take out wedding insurance
- Draft guest list
- Decide on wedding party
- Book reception venue
- Create wedding spreadsheet
- Create wedding email address
- Caterers and menus
- Wedding dress
- Groom's outfit and grooming
- Dress and suit fittings
- Hair and makeup and trials
- Wedding stationery
- Photographer
- Videographer
- Wedding party outfits
- Wedding cake
- Florist

How To Plan A Wedding Without Killing Anyone

- Wedding transport
- Entertainment
- Music or DJ
- Wedding rings
- Honeymoon, visas and travel insurance
- Wedding website (if having one)
- Order of service
- Readers for ceremony
- Witnesses for ceremony
- Wedding gift list
- Decor
- Wedding day favours or gifts
- Readings
- Music
- Seating plan
- Photo list for photographer
- Send out confirmation email to all suppliers for peace of mind
- Write a rough plan of the actual day's timings

Chapter Three

Wedding Spreadsheet

A wedding spreadsheet is an ideal way to get organised. It gives a greater degree of flexibility when it comes to things that change frequently like the budget, guest list, and seating plan by allowing you to change things without making your beautiful handwritten notes look like a scribbled illegible mess. A spreadsheet also means that you can easily print out up to date sheets for your wedding planner, if like me you like to have a physical copy of the information.

Suggested Tabs include:

- Budget
- Ceremony or Day guests
- Reception or Evening guests
- Seating plan
- Thank-you and gift list

How To Plan A Wedding Without Killing Anyone

Budget

This tab is pretty self-explanatory. It's a good idea to include all of your anticipated incomings in one column and total it up at the bottom using simple formula or a calculator. In a separate column include all your anticipated expenses and again total it up at the bottom using simple formula or a calculator.

Then subtract your expenses total from your incomings total to find if your incomings cover your expenses. An example of this is shown in the table below. Chapter four will look more in detail at what costs to include in your budget.

Incomings		Expenses	
Savings	100	Venue	100
Her parents	100	Rings	100
His parents	100	Cake	100
Future savings	100	Flowers	100
Total	400	Total	400
Incomings-expenses = 400-400 = 0			

This table is obviously a massive oversimplification - if only weddings were this straightforward!

Wedding Spreadsheet

If your incomings don't cover your expenses, you'll need to either find more cash to cover the cost or make some cut backs.

> **Top Tip**
>
> Simple spreadsheets and maths formulas can save a lot of time.

Ceremony/day guests

This tab will cover the details of all the people you intend to invite to your ceremony. Each horizontal row can start with the guest's name. You can then add different columns to keep track of whatever information you need alongside each person's name. These columns can include:

- Postal or email addresses
- Invite sent?
- RSVP
- Starter choice
- Main choice
- Dessert choice
- Dietary requirements

Reception/evening guests

This tab will cover the details of all the people you intend to invite to your reception. Similar to the previous tab you can add columns with relevant information alongside the guest's names.

"Operate from love"
-Gina Rodriguez

Wedding Spreadsheet

Please feel free to have as many guest tabs as you do separate invite lists. Keeping them on separate tabs makes it easier to keep track.

Seating plan

Some advocate using sticky notes and a giant sheet of paper for the seating plan (see Chapter twenty-two for more help with seating plans) which sounds fun, if not a little like hard work involving a lot of paper and requiring a lot of free space. I found the spreadsheet ideal. With a simple click of a button I could move people around, changing my mind over and over again.

To do this I created a column under each table number or name and then added names below each one, clicking and moving them around as I wished.

Thank-you list

This is more useful for after the wedding but an unbelievably useful idea. As you open gifts and cards, keep a list of all your guests and what gift you received from them. Then when you come to write your thank-you cards it isn't one huge

> **Top Tip**
>
> To save time writing them all out again, just copy over the names of your guests from the guest list tabs.

memory test and you don't end up looking like horribly ungrateful people.

Furthermore, as you write and send your thank-you cards you can mark people off the list (I simply coloured the box a friendly green colour). This helps make sure you don't forget to send anyone a thank you.

Other admin

I would also recommend setting up a joint wedding email and bank account. Make sure to use your wedding email address when giving contact details to suppliers and for RSVPs. This will help you both keep track of wedding correspondence, preventing your wedding emails from getting lost in everyday correspondence and junk mail. Similarly, a joint bank account will help you both keep track of and control spending.

Wedding Spreadsheet

Summary

- A good wedding spreadsheet can help massively with organisation, especially where large numbers of guests are involved.

- Must-have tabs include: Budget, Guest lists, Seating Plan and a Thank You and gift list.

- Feel free to add any tabs that help with your organisation.

- It's also a great idea to set up joint wedding email and bank accounts to help keep organised.

Wedmin

Email
Email address: ....
Password hint: ....

Bank Details
Bank account Number: ....
Bank account Sort Code: ....
Online username: ....
Password hint: ....
Memorable word hint: ....

Wedding Insurance Details

....
....
....
....

Chapter Four

The Budget

It's a big and to be frank not that fun (actually not fun at all) part of wedding planning, but it is essential. I would suggest setting out the budget ought to be your first major wedding task as it's helpful to be realistic from the start regarding what you have available funds-wise. It's also good to be on the same page as your partner in terms of what you envisage spending.

The average UK wedding costs about £30,000 (2019). Try not to let this figure shock you as it's obviously perfectly possible to spend a lot less or a lot more. Interestingly statistics show that the more a couple spend on their wedding, the more likely they are to get divorced, so please don't see this as a target amount. Weddings come in all shapes and sizes and it's important to remember that a wedding is a day whereas a marriage lasts a lifetime (hopefully). That said, there is no correct amount to spend on a wedding and whatever you spend some will consider it way too much and others not enough. This isn't about pleasing others; it's about spending what's right for you and your partner

First think about how you will pay for the wedding, typical funds come from:

- Personal savings you already have
- Relatives
- Future savings you can set aside

Make a realistic plan for what you can set aside for the wedding whilst you are planning it. Don't be unrealistic in your savings targets, as this will only add to the stress of wedding planning. Total up these amounts, perhaps in your wedding spreadsheet as suggested in Chapter Three.

Try not to take out loans or credit cards to pay for your wedding, if avoidable. Debt can be a major cause of stress and in fact divorce, so it pays not to start your married life in debt. A smaller wedding that you can afford is, in my opinion, a much better idea than a larger wedding that you can't. That said, it's entirely your choice and finance is of course an option. If you do choose this option, make sure to research thoroughly to minimise the amount you'll be paying back in

> **Top Tip**
>
> The key figure is what you have to spend, work out a figure and stick to it. Try not to be tempted to spend more.

The Budget

interest. I'm no Martin Lewis, but there are ways to borrow money which end up costing less in the long run.

Once you have an estimate of the funds available, keep this figure in mind as you fill in your expenses budget.

The table below is a guide to setting out your budget, with the various costs separated out alongside how much the average couple (2017) spends on them. Try to use this as a guide together to fill in the expenses column of your wedding spreadsheet. Remember it is better to over-estimate and be left with excess funds than to underestimate and be caught short.

In brackets I've included what my now husband and I spent (2017) just as a reminder that these typical costs are flexible. We simply didn't have £30,000 to spend on our wedding so we made it work and still had an absolutely phenomenal and unforgettable day. To do this we prioritised things that mattered most to us over things that didn't. For example, we had a bit of a blow-out on the ties for the

> **Top Tip**
>
> Don't be afraid to ask for help. We literally had no budget for a honeymoon, so asked guests to contribute to our honeymoon fund instead of buying wedding gifts. This worked perfectly with some guests doing so and others explaining they'd prefer to buy a present. We ended up with a dream honeymoon and some wonderful presents too!

groom and groomsmen which my husband designed himself. We are also fortunate to have wonderful friends who we could have frank conversations with about costs. The groomsmen wore black suits they all already owned, which they all looked dashing in, and the bridesmaids paid for their own dresses.

Where there's a will there's a way: if you're honest with those around you, you can afford to get married on any budget. As The Knack once told us:

"You can't put a price on love"

"A Wedding is a day; a marriage is a lifetime"

-unknown

How To Plan A Wedding Without Killing Anyone

Expense	Budget Allocation	Typical UK Cost £
Engagement Party		500 (150)
Venue(s)		6000 (3766)
Catering – food and drink		5000 (0)
Favours		175 (50)
Transport		500 (356)
Accommodation		300 (200)
Rings		800 (155)
Wedding Stationery		400 (80)
Florist		800 (525)
Décor		1000 (828)
Entertainment		750 (400)
Music – Band or DJ		750 (0)
Photographer		1000 (675)
Videographer		1000 (250)
Cake		500 (330)
Dress and alterations		1350 (620)
Veil		150 (5)
Shoes		150 (25)
Lingerie		125 (54)
Jewellery		175 (45)
Bridesmaids' outfits		500 (0)
Hair and make up		400 (230)
Nails		75 (50)
Suit(s)		500 (300)
Ties		100 (400)
Insurance		30 (25)
Postage		100 (60)
Attendants' outfits		500 (0)
Registrar		550 (543)

The Budget

Notice of Marriage	70 (70)
Rehearsal dinner	600 (500)
Gifts for bridal party	400 (200)
Hen and stag do	500 (280)
Honeymoon	3750 (0)
Contingency	500
Total	**28,000 (11,172)**

<u>Bringing down the cost</u>

There are various ways to help bring down cost of a wedding, especially when the budget is tight:

1. Pick an unconventional season or even day of the week. Picking a Friday or Sunday can half venue costs, and Monday to Thursday can lower them even further. This may not always be a popular choice with guests.
2. Reduce the number of guests – option one can help with this.
3. Get friends and family to help – utilise their talents. My parents helped make our invites and this saved us a great deal of money.
4. Skip the wedding favours – many guests won't even notice there aren't any as they often get left behind on the day anyway.
5. Instead of hiring expensive wedding cars, if a friend or relative has a nice car they may be able to help.
6. Haggle, be honest with suppliers about your budget and don't be afraid to ask for a discount. The price

you are quoted the first time can almost always be negotiated down.
7. Speak to the florist about using in-season flowers that are grown in the UK, rather than paying extra to import out of season flowers from abroad. I loved the look of Dahlias, but these were out-of-season and expensive. My wonderful florist recommended a much cheaper double-headed Chrysanthemum which she could source locally. I honestly couldn't tell the difference (florist blasphemy sorry!)
8. Look at hiring a newer photographer and/or videographer who will work for lower rates in return for experience. Our videographer was relatively new to the wedding video business and so gave us a hefty discount, but still did a phenomenal job.
9. If you can't afford an expensive tiered cake there are other options for example M&S sell individual tiers you can decorate yourself.
10. You can buy amazing wedding dresses from more affordable shops such as Wed2Be. High street stores have also started offering their own wedding lines for almost unbelievably reasonable prices.
11. There are some beautiful veils available to buy on eBay for less than £10.
12. Many brides spend a fortune on uncomfortable shoes that nobody even sees. Another option is to buy a cheap but comfortable pair of ballet pumps and even decorate them yourself.

The Budget

13. Bridesmaid outfits don't need to be bought from expensive boutique shops. There are beautiful dresses available both online and on the high street. If buying online from abroad there are even Facebook groups (for example China Wedding dresses) which allow you to check out other's purchases before committing.
14. Hair and makeup – although I wouldn't recommend doing it yourself (shaky hands can make eye liner impossible) if you have a friend or relative who works in this area don't be afraid to ask for a favour.
15. Shopping outlets are ideal for finding cut-price but still top-quality suits.
16. Cheap stamps can be bought in bulk on eBay – this can save a fortune on postage.
17. Don't be afraid to DIY where you want to, personal touches add a lot to a wedding. I made our wedding signs, our wine charm favours and candle holders and people loved all the personal touches.
18. A sit-down three-course meal can be expensive, keep costs down by looking at other food options such as buffets.

There are so many ways to have a wonderful day whatever your budget – so don't despair if everything seems completely unaffordable initially. The main point of this chapter is to help you move past the "Oh my goodness! How much?" stage of thinking and into the, "I will do this my way" stage.

How To Plan A Wedding Without Killing Anyone

Summary

- First total up the money available to you to plan the wedding with.

- Draw up a budget, with your funds available in mind.

- If your expenses exceed your funds available, try to prioritise and reduce spending in your budget where you can.

- Remember, the amount of money you spend doesn't make a wedding or a marriage.

The Budget

Budget

Incomings	Outgoings

Chapter Five

The Location/venue(s)

Choosing your wedding location is such an exciting and key task when it comes to wedding planning. Most couples tend to choose either:

a) A place of significance to them as a couple
b) A location which is easy for friends and family to get to
c) Somewhere entirely new, creating a new special place.

Obviously, a location can fit into more than just one of these categories.

> **Top Tip**
>
> Find a venue you both love, don't be afraid to hold out for this, when you find it, you'll know!

The Location/venue(s)

Picking a Venue(s)

When a location has been decided upon, it is then time to decide the venue or venues. The two key venues are:

1) The venue at which your ceremony will be held, for example a church, registry office or any premises approved to hold marriages or civil ceremonies.
2) The venue at which your reception will be held

Some people choose to have their ceremony and reception in the same venue. This can simplify things in terms of transporting guests between the two venues but may not be possible for some venues.

It's worth also considering at this point where you'll get ready on the morning of the big day. Ideally the bridal preparation room will have enough space to accommodate bridesmaids, hair and make-up artists as well as your photographer(s) and videographer. Preparation will always be more fun and relaxed if everyone has a reasonable amount of personal space.

> **Top Tip**
>
> Consider the rough number of guests you would like to invite and the size of wedding you desire and have this in mind when picking a venue. If you want a small wedding with 30 or so guests, you'll need a very different venue to someone with 300 guests.

I chose to get ready in the hotel we were getting married in, I can be a worrier so decided this would reduce the potential stress of getting to the ceremony on time. The hotel let us use the bridal suite which was huge and had its own en-suite – ideal for lots of nervous and excited ladies!

If it's doable financially, I would recommend booking a large hotel room as close as possible to the ceremony location. On top of the reasons above, it's your big day so the perfect time to treat yourself and your bridal party.

If you're getting ready at home, this too can be a very special experience. A familiar environment can be very calming when your nerves are a little frayed so there are definite up-sides to this option too. Do whatever works for you!

<u>Picking a Date</u>

When picking a date, you have two main decisions:

1) The time of year   2) The day of the week

Some people will choose a date that holds a special significance, for example an anniversary or lucky number.

When choosing a season and time of year think about what you want from your wedding day. If you would like an outdoor ceremony and reception, the depths of winter might not be a popular choice amongst guests. On the other hand, out of season weddings can be a lot cheaper when booking both venues and suppliers.

The Location/venue(s)

Personally, I hate being hot and sweaty in photos and we wanted a mostly indoor wedding so a November wedding was ideal both in terms of what we wanted and cost-wise.

When choosing a day of the week, bear in mind that people often assume weddings will take place on Saturdays and can moan if you choose other days of the week as it means they'll likely have to take time off work. On the other hand, venues often offer Friday or Saturday weddings for discounts of up to 50%, with even higher discounts on other weekdays. If you're happy to get married on a day other than a Saturday, there are big savings to be had. This compromise can free up budget for other areas. Furthermore, if a guest isn't prepared to take a day off for your wedding, I would question how close they are to you and whether or not I would personally want them there.

It is also worth remembering that popular days in wedding seasons (Saturdays during the summer months and other seasonal Holidays especially) can book up early both in terms of venue and suppliers. This means that if you want these dates you will likely need to plan much further in advance.

It's all about prioritising and choosing what works best for you and your fiancé when it comes to venue and date. It is worth checking the availability of people you definitely want to attend – it's no use booking your wedding during the same month your sister is due to give birth, and then complaining when she says she can't make it.

> *"Any home can be a castle, when the King and Queen are in love"*
>
> -unknown

The Location/venue(s)

Religious ceremonies

If you'd like a religious ceremony it's best to get in touch with your religious leader as soon as possible to arrange a time to discuss desired dates and so on. The religious leader (some even have event coordinators) can then help you schedule your big day along with the availability of those you want involved – for example an organist – and your reception venue availability.

Talk to your point of contact about any requirements for being married in the place of worship you have chosen. Different religions and even different denominations of individual religions will have different requirements and it is essential to know what these are if you are to meet them.

Civil ceremonies

Civil ceremonies in the UK cannot have any reference to religion in them at any point. There are lots of horror stories on the internet about them enforcing this rule to extreme levels; I read one lady was told she couldn't walk down the aisle to Halo by Beyoncé. From my experience, if you're unsure then call the registry office and ask. When I asked about Halo, my registry office couldn't see an issue – but definitely worth checking!

Booking the venue and registrar can seem like a chicken and egg issue. You don't want to book the venue and find out the registrar has no slots that day, but equally you don't want to book the registrar and find out your venue is already booked that day. I recommend the following:

1) Choose your date
2) Check with your venue regarding availability for this day. When a date is agreed, explain to them that you are going to book the registrar and then will call back to place your deposit for the venue.
3) Call the registrar and book the registrar (2pm is a fairly typical time to book for – but do think about your rough day plan when picking a time).
4) Call the venue and put your deposit down on the venue.

I recommend doing all of this over one day or ideally a weekend.

Once the actual wedding itself is booked, sit back, relax and give yourselves the night off. This is such an integral part of wedding planning and you've sorted it! I recommend celebrating in some way – perhaps a wedding-planning free night.

<u>Wedding Insurance</u>

Once the date and location are set, book your wedding insurance. Wedding insurance doesn't cost much, but gives you peace of mind and protects you from circumstances

The Location/venue(s)

beyond your control as a couple. Always read the policy to see what you are covered for and pick the insurance best suited for your wedding and budget.

How To Plan A Wedding Without Killing Anyone

Summary

- Decide upon a location, i.e. area of the country, first.

- Once you have a location, choose your location(s) for your ceremony and reception.

- When choosing a date consider the time of year, and day of the week as well as the availability of key guests.

- Religious and Civil ceremonies have different requirements – make sure you meet these and their deadlines.

- Always get wedding insurance.

The Location/venue(s)

Venue Ideas

Venues

Morning of the Wedding (Bride)
Address:

....
....

Morning of the Wedding (Groom)
Address:

....
....

Ceremony
Address:

....
....

Time: ....

Reception
Address:

....
....

Time: ....

Chapter Six

Wedding-planning-free Days

Wedding-planning-free days are essential to keep your sanity during the wedding planning process. I laughed at the idea when I came across it when we first started wedding planning – mocking the idea of couples who would do nothing but talk about their upcoming wedding.

I now hold my hands up and admit how wrong I was. A combination of excitement and having lots to get done (especially when planning over a shorter time frame) means that

---

Top Tip

If you're both getting stressed and snappy with each other, take a day off. Wedding planning can be stressful but it doesn't have to be! Refresh and come back to it when you feel restored and rejuvenated after a nice break. This way you will enjoy the process much more!

inevitably we ended up having wedding-planning discussions almost, if not every day. In the evenings, after work, we would cram tasks in. On the weekend each day would have a task assigned. Even when we weren't doing it, we'd still be talking about it.

It soon became clear we needed to assign days where we would not talk about wedding planning, which we did. I seemed to struggle most with these days! What made it easier and more fun was when we planned something to do.

Furthermore, wedding planning can bring about disagreements as a couple and new levels of stress. Wedding planning free days spent doing something as a couple which you both enjoy can help remind you what the wedding planning process is all about. It can seem wedding planning is all about organising the best and most perfect wedding day whilst impressing all your friends and family - and keeping within a budget that at times seems impossible.

Spending time with your partner, away from wedding planning, reminds you that a wedding is actually a celebration of a lifelong commitment to your best friend, life partner and soulmate. It can remind you that what really matters is how much you love this person and spending time with them and how lucky you are to have found them. In comparison to the importance of this, your wedding day doesn't seem so central.

On top of this, after you're married, if you've done nothing but wedding plan for months it can feel a little strange and

> "Time is free but it is priceless"
> -unknown

take time to remember what you used to talk about before you started wedding planning. If you've had wedding planning free days throughout, this is less likely to be an issue.

At first, it can seem like you've forgotten what you used to do before wedding-planning. Think back to what you both enjoy doing together. A few suggestions include:

- Cinema
- Netflix and takeaway
- Dinner out
- Exercise together
- Day trips
- Board games
- Dinner parties
- Bowling
- Walking or hiking
- Take a class together for example a dance class or cookery class
- Cook together
- A holiday
- Spa day

In your wedding planner, write a list of your own activity ideas, as we all have different interests and it can be great to have a list to come back to when you're struggling for ideas.

If you're struggling not to talk about wedding planning a fun solution can be a swear jar. Each time either of you

Wedding-planning-free Days

mentions anything wedding-related on a wedding planning free day then you place a fine in the jar. As a bonus, this jar can help fund wedding-planning free day activities.

How To Plan A Wedding Without Killing Anyone

Summary

- It's important to take time away from wedding planning.

- Do things you and your partner enjoy together.

- Write a list of these activities in advance, so you're not short of ideas on the day.

- Introduce a swear jar for any mention of wedding planning.

Wedding planning free day - activity ideas

Chapter Seven

The Wedding/Bridal Party

The wedding party consists of the bride and groom (or brides or grooms) along with all the other major roles people play in your wedding. This can be a complex part of wedding planning both in terms of knowing which roles there are to fill and trying to minimise offence when filling them whilst still having the people you want.

This chapter will first explain the different traditional roles along with the duties they typically entail – though bear in mind this is all up to you as a couple. It could be argued that tradition is just peer pressure from dead people and while some of us love tradition, nothing is compulsory. Try to use tradition as a suggestion, and make it work for you as a couple – if it's not working, don't hesitate to find your own way instead!

The chapter will then look at ways you can ask people to fulfil these roles and your duty to them.

The Wedding/Bridal Party

Traditional roles

Bride's side

- Father of the Bride
    - Helps plan and complete pre-wedding tasks
    - Walking the bride down the aisle
    - Speech and toast at the reception
    - Father-daughter dance
    - Helps host the wedding

- Mother of the Bride
    - Helps plan and complete pre-wedding tasks
    - Often helps the bride and bridesmaids get ready on the morning of
    - Helps host the wedding

- Maid or matron of honour
    - Bride's right-hand man or woman
    - Emotional support
    - Help with pre-wedding tasks
    - Keeps the bridesmaids in check
    - Plans the hen do and bridal shower
    - Sign marriage licence
    - Holds the bridal bouquet when required
    - Adjusts bride's train when necessary
    - Helps host

- Bridesmaids
    - Support team for the bride

- - Support the maid of honour
  - Help with pre-wedding tasks

- Junior bridesmaids

Groom's side

- Father of the Groom
  - Helps plan and complete pre-wedding tasks
  - Helps host the rehearsal (often the wedding too now)

- Mother of the Groom
  - Helps plan and complete pre-wedding tasks
  - Helps host the rehearsal (often the wedding too now)

- Best man
  - Groom's right-hand man or woman
  - Emotional support
  - Help with pre-wedding tasks
  - Keeps the groomsmen in check
  - Plans the stag or bachelor party
  - Sign marriage licence
  - Keeps the rings safe
  - Helps host
  - Gives a speech and toast

- Groomsmen

The Wedding/Bridal Party

- - Support team for the groom
  - Support the best man
  - Help with pre-wedding tasks
  - Often groomsmen double as ushers i.e. fulfil both roles

- Junior groomsmen

- Ushers
  - Help guests to their seats

- Junior ushers

There are also the roles of the ring bearer and flower girl or child or pet who walk down the aisle first. The ring bearer carries a small cushion with two rings tied to it. These are usually not the actual rings for obvious reasons! The flower child then follows scattering petals from a small basket as they walk down the aisle, ideally looking adorable whilst doing so. They do say never work with children or animals though – so be prepared for this not to go exactly to plan. Some of the funniest wedding videos I've seen have involved temperamental children!

Please remember that the key to all these roles and responsibilities is that they are flexible i.e. not set in stone. If you want your best friend as your maid of honour and that best friend is a guy – so what, as long as you and your partner are happy with this then go for it!

Furthermore, if you want your mum to give a speech rather than your dad, that's absolutely fine too. I just found it useful to know what was traditionally expected when making my decisions so that I would know if any little extra conversations were needed. For example, many people experience the controversial issue of who will walk them down the aisle – no-one, their mum, their biological dad, their step-dad or even someone else entirely. There is nothing wrong with picking whoever feels right for you, but when you know that someone might be a little disappointed with your choice it means you can speak to them and try to resolve painful issues before they arise.

> **Top Tip**
>
> Your day will be much more special and relaxed if you surround yourself with the people you actually want to have around you on your big day. Don't be afraid to be honest with people about this. If they don't understand, you're likely better off without them!

In terms of numbers, this is also flexible – have as many or as few attendants as you want – it's you and your partner's day. Just think through practicalities like getting larger groups of people together (in terms of availability), how many people you want with you when you're getting ready, how big the ceremony room will be and go with what feels right.

The Wedding/Bridal Party

Who to ask

I recommend asking close friends and family members who you enjoy spending time with. Do not ask people out of a feeling of obligation. This will only lead to stress further down the line when you have to deal with a difficult wedding party member who probably didn't really want the role in the first place but felt obliged to accept it.

Try to pick people you know will be good at the task, don't set them up to fail. If you have two close friends, one is amazingly organised and on top of everything and another struggling to balance her daily life already then do everyone a favour and have the former as your maid of honour and the later as your bridesmaid.

How to ask

Asking people to be part of your wedding party can be really exciting. There are lots of ideas on Pinterest around how to do this, ranging from popping a balloon with the question written on a slip of paper inside to candy rings and gift boxes. I went with cupcakes with rice paper "Will you be my bridesmaid?" discs on them which I found on eBay. They went down a treat – as cupcakes always do!

"Choose people who lift you up"

-Michelle Obama

The Wedding/Bridal Party

What if they say no?

If someone says no, try not to assume it's because they hate you and don't want to be part of your big day. There are a whole host of very valid reasons someone might have for saying no, even if they don't share them. A few very valid reasons (because I'm sure you're struggling to think of any if you're in this situation) might include:

> **Top Tip**
>
> If someone turns you down, don't react out of anger. Try to think with compassion and understanding and see things from their point of view. Ask questions calmly to try to understand if you need to.

- The person might be pregnant and due on the day of your wedding, but not be quite ready to open up about the pregnancy just yet
- The person might be struggling with health issues they haven't opened up about yet, physical or mental
- The person might genuinely not be able to afford the cost that comes with being part of a wedding

If someone values you enough to be honest and say they can't commit to being your bridesmaid (or whatever role you have invited them to take) this is a million times better than them committing and then doing a really rubbish job and letting you down. Feel free to let them know you're disappointed, maybe even ask why to see if there's anything you can help with, but at the end of the day it's not worth losing a friend over!

Your responsibilities to members of the wedding party

It is essential to remember that not all members of the wedding party will have attended many weddings before, and some may not even have read this book!? Therefore, be aware that they may not actually know their responsibilities and work to resolve this.

Before I got engaged and married, one of my dearest friends asked me to be her maid of honour. I was over the moon, filled to the brim with excitement for what I knew would be an amazing day. After the initial thrill I soon realised I actually knew nothing about weddings (a feeling which I struggle to remember now!) and had no idea what this actually meant. I googled maid of honour duties and made notes – but everywhere I looked suggested something different. It was very confusing.

A few weeks later, my friend and I sat down and she explained to me what she needed me to do. It was a massive relief and was great because it meant I would be the maid of honour that she wanted.

I therefore recommend talking to member of the wedding party and letting them know explicitly what you would like from them. None of them will want to let you down (unless

The Wedding/Bridal Party

you've chosen horribly) so this is the ideal way to make sure everyone is on the same page.

In terms of who is expected to pay for what, be clear from the outset. These conversations can be awkward if left until the last minute as there's lots of conflicting suggestions online and it can often be confusing.

Usually whoever is paying for the wedding covers the cost of flowers whereas outfits, accessories, shoes, hair and make-up are often up for discussion. I would recommend perhaps a compromise whereby the bridal party pay for their own outfits but you cover the costs of hair and make-up or vice versa. The wedding party (the bridesmaids for the bride and the groomsmen for the groom) usually cover the cost of hen and stag dos.

How To Plan A Wedding Without Killing Anyone

Summary

- Weddings tend to have a list of traditional roles and associated responsibilities.

- Feel free to do your own thing.

- Asking people can be exciting, but don't be too let down if they say no.

- Be clear around what you expect from your wedding party.

The Wedding/Bridal Party

Wedding Party

Father of the bride..
Mother of the bride..
Maid of honour..
Bridesmaids...
....
....
....
Junior bridesmaids..

Father of the groom...
Mother of the groom..
Best man..
Groomsmen...
....
....
....
Junior groomsmen..
Ushers..
Junior ushers...

Ring bearer...
Flower person..

69

Chapter Eight

The Wedding Website

Creating a wedding website is an easy way of communicating all the need-to-know wedding information with your guests. Including all of this information in the invitation can often take up too much space, especially if it's a simple invite you're going for. Furthermore, fielding the same questions over and over again from guests who have inevitably lost their invite can be tiring and challenging if you can't remember all the details off the top of your head. Your simple solution: the wedding website. The FAQs of your big day, all in one easy-to-access place.

Which site?

There are several sites which offer free services specifically tailored to setting up your own wedding website. They are all designed to be simple to use, given that the majority of brides and grooms aren't proficient in website design or coding. A few highly recommended (all free of charge, some with optional chargeable extras) sites include:

- Joy
- The Knot
- Wedding wire
- Luv birds
- My Wedding
- eWedding

For the more confident website builders or those who want a less wedding specific website with a bit more versatility, try the following free general website builders:

- Wix
- Squarespace
- Weebly

I personally used TheKnot and found it very easy to follow. I simply picked a template then filled in our relevant information in the ready set-out sections. It wasn't a ground-breaking or a super original website but it had all the information our guests needed in a pretty and easy to use format.

> **Top Tip**
>
> Password protect your website to prevent wedding crashers and unwanted guests finding out all the key information online and turning up unexpectedly on your big day.

What information to include

As mentioned earlier, the wedding website ideally serves as a FAQ for your wedding. Split this information into natural sections and pages on your website to make it easy for your guests to find what they are looking for. Suggested sections include:

- How we met story
- Proposal story
- Where and when the wedding will take place
- Wedding party – who's who
- How to get there and transport details
- Accommodation recommendations
- Things to do in the local area
- Details of any other wedding events you're organising
- Menus
- RSVP
- Dress code
- Gift registry

You can include anything you like on your wedding website – personalise it and make it your own. This and your invites will be the first impression guests get of your wedding. Try to make it in keeping with the feel you and your partner want for the day - for example, if it's a beach wedding, why not use a classy looking beach and waves template.

"The best things in life aren't things"

-unknown

How To Plan A Wedding Without Killing Anyone

To make your website more personal, try to include a few photos of the two of you. Engagement photos are wonderful for wedding websites, your guests are all coming together to celebrate you both as a couple, so help get them even more excited than they already are!

Facebook group

The month before the wedding, I also decided to create a Facebook event. I read this tip in a Facebook bridal group and it worked a treat for last-minute organisation. This might not seem very classy, but I prefer to think of it as being modern and technologically proficient.

> **Top Tip**
>
> Create a wedding hashtag for guests to use when uploading photos across different social media platforms – it will make it much easier for you to find them all #goodidea.

The Facebook group is ideal for ensuring guests are aware of crucial last-minute information. For example, our wedding was held a short taxi ride from the local train station where most of our friends would be arriving. Taxis had to be booked in advance and I was sure some would not realise this, despite it being on our website and me telling everyone many times. I therefore reminded everyone of this crucial piece of information in the Facebook group and it worked a treat!

The Wedding Website

I also shared a brief timeline of the day on the Facebook group the week before. This served to whip up excitement and informed guests of practicalities and key information, like when they would be being fed. Put yourself in the mind of your guest and ask yourself what you would want to know in advance.

How To Plan A Wedding Without Killing Anyone

Summary

- A wedding website can save you a lot of time answering guests' questions – simply direct them to your website.

- Use a free, wedding-specific website builder – they don't take much, if any, IT proficiency!

- Password protect the website if you can.

- Consider a Facebook group for last-minute organisation.

Website

For us
Username: ....
Password: ....

Website Ideas:
....
....
....
....
....
....
....
....
....

For guests:
Website address: ....
Website password: ....

Chapter Nine

The Guest List

The guest list can be a controversial topic. Most likely your venue choice or budget will limit the number of guests you can invite. This isn't a bad thing, as you likely chose your venue with this ambience in mind. Some might want a massive wedding with a thousand guests whereas other might feel happiest with ten of their closest friends and family. There is no correct guest list or size!

If the guest list is getting on top of you and it all seems too intense, just remember that your wedding is a commitment between you and your partner and that is the most important part. Ideally you will be surrounded by friends and family who love and support the both of you. This doesn't <u>have</u> to include your Great Uncle Sam who you've met possibly once when you were days old! You are in control of your guest list, whatever this means to you - whether it is you choosing as a couple, leaving your partner in charge or letting someone else entirely decide.

The Guest List

Ceremony/reception guests

When planning our wedding we had 60 spots for the ceremony and wedding breakfast (the room capacity) and 60 extra spots for the evening reception. When it came to the guest list, I felt really uncomfortable inviting people only to the evening. I was concerned they would feel like second class friends. In fact, they didn't at all – many of them were married themselves (or in the process of planning a wedding) and understood the guest number predicament – instead they were touched that we wanted them to be a part of one of the most special days of our lives. My advice is just to be honest with people. After family and the bridal party, we only had room for 11 other guests each meaning basically 5 friends plus partners. I explained this to friends who were evening guests, whose main response was confusion as to why I was explaining myself.

> **Top Tip**
>
> The Bride and Groom usually count in the guest numbers – don't forget to clarify this with your venue!

Family pressures

In days gone by, the bride's family took charge of the guest list. Given they tended to pay for the wedding in its entirety, there was often little the couple could say or do. Speaking to my mum and her friends, they had little, if any, say regarding the guest list. My mum recounts this consisted mainly of her father's friends, which is something she didn't want for us. Bear in mind that some parents may still be clinging to this tradition. If this is the case, but you want to decide your own guest list, perhaps let them down gently.

In term of family guests, fairness is often an issue. Rarely are both families of the exact same size. This can lead to challenges when the "side" with the larger family only has numbers to invite siblings, but the "side" with the smaller family may have numbers to invite distant cousins. Arguably, one way of sorting this is to allocate numbers based upon how close you are to these family members. My now-husband grew up with his two cousins and described them as being like brothers – so much so that he had them both as groomsmen. In contrast, I felt closer to some cousins than others, so perhaps controversially invited some but not others.

> ### Top Tip
>
> As a general rule, don't invite people who aren't invited to the wedding to other events such as engagement parties, showers and hen/stag parties. And if you do, be really clear that they aren't invited to the actual wedding.

Other pressures

Please sit down for this section, it will likely come as quite a shock – it certainly did for me! In all probability, at least one person who you haven't spoken to in over ten years is going to get in touch asking for an invite. Why would they think they'd be invited? Why would they even want to come? How do you tell them they're not invited? These are all questions that will race through your mind. As well as the classic of whether you're a horrible person for forgetting about them.

Let's begin:

1. You are not a horrible person at all – would you expect to be invited to someone's wedding who you haven't even spoken to in said period of time?
2. People can be selfish and self-absorbed and not realise how ridiculous they are being.
3. They probably don't care about your wedding, but are interested in a free meal and party.
4. My suggested reply is something along the lines of – "Hey, hope you're well? - haven't spoken in so long! We're keeping our wedding pretty small, so we're only able to invite our very closest family and friends. I'm sorry that we can't extend an invitation and I really hope you can understand".

If you feel like you want to reconnect and invite them, then that's great but do not feel pressured into inviting them and do not feel bad about saying no. Try to be reassured that you're not the only one experiencing this seemingly weird phenomenon!

There will likely also be people you know and like, but either don't want at your wedding or don't have space for. If

How To Plan A Wedding Without Killing Anyone

"I run my world"

-Beyoncé

this is the case then the above explanation works too. If they are truly your friend, they will completely understand and accept this explanation. If not, then you've weeded out someone that didn't really deserve your friendship anyway!

Who to invite

There are several hilarious flow charts online for whom to invite or not invite. Do check these out for a laugh! My main advice for the guest list is to do what feels right and try not to be pressured into inviting people you don't want there – either by others or by your own guilt. My recommended steps, with an example of sixty-day guests:

> **Top Tip**
>
> Don't forget to include partners and plus ones in the guest list, if you intend to invite them.

Guest List	Day Guests = 60
You and your partner!	Day = 60 - 2 = 58
Family you want to invite – for example parents, siblings, grandparents, aunts, uncles, cousins	Day = 58 – 20 = 38
Bridal Party and partners	Day = 38 – 18 = 20
Friends – divide the number left between two	20/2 = 10 friends each

The rest of your friends can be invited as evening guests. I was surprised how numbers add up so quickly (that sounds ridiculous, I know!). Initially 60 sounded like so many places, I remember thinking to myself, "Gosh, I'm not that popular!". But especially when partners are included, the numbers add up quickly!

Some people choose to allocate a few guests for their parents to pick i.e. their friends. This is a nice touch, though, as with everything, completely up to you!

Handling guest upgrades

Ideally you can send out just the day invites (ceremony and wedding breakfast) first, then get the RSVPs back. This allows you to then take stock of guest numbers and invite a few more people (upgrade) if you have space left over from those who can't make it.

Sometimes, however, time is tight and all the invites, day and evening, go out at the same time. This will inevitably lead to a few awkward conversations. Personally, we were honest with a few close friends from the outset explaining our number limitations and that if there was anyone couldn't make it to the ceremony then they would be first on our list. As it happens, we did upgrade several people. It's all in the framing; explain to them how happy you would be to have them there and so on.

The Guest List

<u>Summary</u>

- The guest list can be controversial with pressure from both family and friends as well as what you feel you should be doing.

- Try to overcome these pressures and focus on inviting the guests you and your partner want to celebrate with you on <u>your</u> special day.

- What may seem like a large number of guests initially can fill up very quickly.

- Be honest with friends and family.

- Upgrading guests can feel embarrassing, but real friends will be excited and happy!

- The following guest list page can easily be included as part of your wedding spreadsheet.

How To Plan A Wedding Without Killing Anyone

Guest List

Name	Contact details	Invite Sent	RSVP	Food choices	Allergies

Chapter Ten

Wedding Stationery

Wedding stationery can often be overlooked and under-budgeted for when planning a wedding. To simplify the wedding stationery confusion, here is a list including the main elements of wedding stationery:

- Engagement party invitations
- Save the dates
- Be my bridesmaid (and other wedding party roles) cards
- Hen and stag party invitations
- Invitations (day and evening if some guests are not invited to the whole day)

> **Top Tip**
>
> If you know a crafty person or feel crafty yourself – DIY wedding stationery can save a lot of money. Remember to be realistic though and don't expect professional service or product from yourself, family members or friends if they are not professionals!

- Rehearsal dinner invitation
- Signage cards (for example buffet choices and directions)
- Order of Service (for the ceremony)
- Reserved seats cards (for the ceremony)
- Place cards (for the wedding breakfast)
- Menus (for the wedding breakfast)
- Table plan (for the wedding breakfast)
- Guest book
- Favour tags
- Thank-you cards

The idea is that you pick your wedding colours and style and then have all the wedding stationery in keeping with this design. The degree to which you do this is, as with everything, completely up to you as a couple. My "Be my bridesmaid" cards were cup cakes with little rice paper toppers and our thank-you cards were photo collages of our honeymoon – neither sticking to the general stationery style but both exactly what we wanted. Others will want everything in their chosen style to provide a sense of cohesion and sleek design. This too is perfect, if that's what you'd prefer.

> **Top Tip**
>
> Some more modern couples are using e-invite sites such as paperlesspost. Though criticised by some traditionalists, a friend used e-invites for her wedding and I was a huge fan. It meant I always had the details to hand on my phone!

"Create your own style"

-Anna Wintour

How To Plan A Wedding Without Killing Anyone

Most of the elements in the list are completely optional – as I keep saying this is your wedding and needs to be personal and what you want. For example, we didn't send save the date cards and just sent the invitations earlier. I originally wrote a large paragraph here explaining this decision – but have since deleted it upon realising I don't have to explain our decision. It was what felt right to us. This applies to you too – do what feels right! That said, it is useful to know what standard practice is in order to make informed decisions.

Save the dates

Save the dates typically include key details of the wedding such as who it's from, the wedding date, location and that a formal invite will follow. These normally sent only to day guests, not to evening or reception-only guests – so if you do decide to send them to all guests, it's a good idea to be clear about this.

> ## Top Tip
>
> The save the date often gives guests the first impressions of what your wedding – try to make it unique and representative of you as a couple.

Typically save the dates are sent 4-6 months before the wedding date itself. However, for destination weddings or those at particularly busy times of year (such as summer, Christmas, Easter holidays or other religious holidays that many of your guests might be celebrating) it might be a good idea to send save the dates eight to twelve months in advance to allow guests more notice.

If your wedding is in a year or two's time, although it can be tempting to send save the dates in all the excitement, don't! Guests will lose save the dates and will likely not have calendars to note the date down in. Worse still, you may change your mind over who you want to invite. Friendship groups change, don't put yourself in the awkward position of having to uninvite someone you grew apart from after sending a save the date several years back.

Invitations

Invitations typically include:

- Whose wedding it is
- Date and time
- Venue(s)
- Reply address and reply card with menu choices if required
- RSVP deadline
- Website details and password

Other important details that can be included on the invite or on the website if invite space is short or the invite is looking too busy:

- Menu choices
- How to get there and maps

- Accommodation suggestions
- Things to do in the area
- Gift list

Try to have all the necessary information on your wedding website so that when guests inevitably lose your invite, they can find all the information they need without you having to repeat it all over again and again!

Usually invitations are sent 6-8 weeks before the wedding date itself. However, as with the save the dates, for destination weddings or those at particularly busy times of year it's a good idea to send invitations 3-4 months in advance to allow guests more notice.

Typically, day and evening guest invitations will look slightly different with different details but will be in the same style. Be clear with guests regarding what they are invited to as confusion will be awkward for both you and them!

Remember to order a few extra invites of both – this is helpful in case you make any mistakes or need to make changes to your guest list. Ordering at a later date can be difficult and pricey! And any spare invites can be kept as mementos.

RSVP deadlines

Don't be surprised by people's tardiness when it comes to RSVPs and deadlines. People have busy lives, try not to take it personally. You will likely find five types of RSVP:

- Those who reply the day or days after they receive your invite. These are people who will never know how grateful you are to them!
- The trickle-in RSVPs over the coming weeks
- The last-minute RSVPs
- The family member who tells you "Oh, I didn't think I had to RSVP because of course I'm coming!" – okay, but what do you want to eat!?
- The still-haven't-replied-by-the-deadline RSVPs

> **Top Tip**
>
> Make it easy for your guests to RSVP – feel free to include reply cards but perhaps also give them an email address or phone number to RSVP to.

This last group is often of a significant size, which can leave you wondering if people just don't want to come. I know I'm dwelling on this, but I promise you their lack of RSVP is almost certainly because people have hectic lives and they forgot they hadn't already sent their RSVP. Some people are also just not that organised and quite laid back, so they don't understand what the big deal is.

How To Plan A Wedding Without Killing Anyone

My in-text top tip (because it's simply that important) is to set the RSVP deadline a week or two before your actual need-to-know deadline. If the venue wants numbers confirmed by the 28th July, set the RSVP deadline at the very latest to the 14th July. This will relieve so much deadline pressure at a time when you don't need added pressure. It also means that on the 14th July (or a few days earlier) you can reasonably chase guests sounding a little panicked, they will hopefully reply feeling awful they left it so late, and you never actually need to be stressed at all.

> Top Tip
>
> Number your RSVP cards and keep a list of who is which number - so that if they come back without a name on, you will know whose RSVP it is.

Spare invites

If you have any extra invites then send them to your favourite celebrities along with a stamped self-addressed envelope and they might just sign it and send it back to you if you're lucky! Some suggestions include:

- Mickey and Minnie Mouse
  The Walt Disney Company
  500 South Buena Vista Street
  Burbank, CA 91521

- Cinderella and Prince Charming
  P.O. Box 1000
  Lake Buena Vista, Florida 32830

- Oprah Winfrey
  Harpo Productions
  PO Box 909715
  Chicago, IL 60690

<u>Other wedding stationery</u>

It can be very easy to become obsessive over everything matching perfectly. For example, we spent weeks trying to find ribbon in a shade of blue which I can now confirm they don't actually make!

Try to remember this is your wedding day and people are there to celebrate you and your partner's love and making of a lifelong commitment to one another. If anyone there, other than the two of you, is bothered by the shade of blue of the table plan not exactly matching that of the invites then they really need to just deal with it and reassess their priorities!

How To Plan A Wedding Without Killing Anyone

Summary

- Wedding stationery is an important but often overlooked part of wedding planning.

- Save the dates are usually sent about 4-6 months prior to the wedding (8-12 for destination weddings or busy times of year).

- Invites are usually sent about 4-6 weeks prior to the wedding (3-4 months for destination weddings or busy times of year).

- Set RSVP deadlines well in advance of actual deadlines to avoid unnecessary stress.

- Don't get too obsessed over wedding stationery – it can often feel much more important than it actually is!

Stationery Checklist

- Engagement party invitations
- Save the dates
- Be my bridesmaid (and other role) cards
- Hen/stag party invitations
- Day invitations
- Evening invitations
- Rehearsal dinner invitations
- Signage cards
  - ....
  - ....
  - ....
  - ....
- Order of Service
- Reserved seats cards
- Place card
- Menu
- Table plan
- Guest book
- Favour tags
- Thank-you cards

Chapter Eleven

Dealing With Difficult People

Weddings tend to bring out the best and worst in people. Most people, myself included, start the wedding planning process assuming everything will be tickety-boo and peachy. Some people exceed these expectations (shout-out to my bridesmaids) whilst others inevitably fall short.

This can be extremely disappointing. You're organising one of the happiest days of your life, and a person who supposedly loves and cares for you is acting in a manner which would perhaps suggest the complete opposite. It's quite easy to sit down, cry and ponder how on earth they think this behaviour is acceptable. This obviously can have

> **Top Tip**
>
> People often project their needs and wants on to you. This isn't necessarily personal, though can feel very hurtful.

quite a negative impact on your experience of the wedding planning process.

This chapter will help you process everything (from the guest who is insistent on bringing the plus-one you didn't invite to the family member who disagrees with every decision you make) and minimise the impact it has on your wedding planning experience.

Change how you think

Eleanor Roosevelt once said *"No one can make you feel inferior without your consent"*. I suggest you apply this idea to the wedding planning process. Aunt Maybel might think it's horrific that you intend to have a fish and chips van instead of a traditional three course dinner after the ceremony. She may be threatening not to attend because of the embarrassment you will cause her and her family. What's important here is how you let Aunt Maybel's opinions and actions impact upon you, and this is entirely your decision. Of course, it's completely ok to be upset and shed a few tears, but it's important not to let it take over. You can achieve this using the following helpful techniques.

> **Top Tip**
>
> Try to communicate how you are feeling with the person concerned. Focus on how you are feeling as a result of their actions – this can reduce confrontation.

How To Plan A Wedding Without Killing Anyone

Try not to over-generalise

Don't come to conclusions based on one person's opinions or preferences. As I've said before, weddings are about you as a couple and sharing a celebration of your love and togetherness with all your friends and family.

That said, it is a good idea to consider whether or not your friends and family will enjoy the day. If you and your partner love spending your holidays on nudist beaches, it might be a bit harsh to enforce a no-clothes dress code on all your guests for the big day.

However, for less extreme hobbies and tastes (no offence intended) there is nothing wrong with expanding your guest's horizons and sharing with them things that mean something to you as a couple. I attended my first ever Ceilidh at a friend's wedding (very embarrassing as I'm actually half Scottish) and absolutely loved it!

The key here is not to over-generalise one person's horror. Just because Aunt Maybel hates the fish and chips van doesn't mean it's unreasonable and everyone will hate it.

This is where your bridal party come in very handy or even other friends and family for that matter; ask them if you're being unreasonable, talk about your ideas and seek reassurance and validation when the vast majority of people love or are at the very least indifferent to the idea.

"No one can make you feel inferior without your consent"

-Eleanor Roosevelt

Avoid using the words should and must

Relatives especially can have a long list of shoulds and musts for you to follow. It's strange because one assumes they went through the same ordeal with their parents and that they would have learned something from this process – oddly this often isn't the case.

Let me be clear, other than the basic rules of society (the law) there aren't any "shoulds" or "musts" on your wedding day. I should wear a white dress, my father must give me away, I should throw my bouquet... I could continue for the rest of this book! Stop here, do away with the words should and must and focus instead on what you would like for your wedding day.

Yes, traditions are wonderful, I personally loved wearing my white dress on my wedding day and felt like an absolute princess, but they are completely optional. It's perfectly acceptable to pick the traditions you like and do away with those you don't. The best part is, you don't even need to explain yourself – you are not on trial for committing a crime because you decide not to toss the bouquet.

I would recommend a swear jar for the words should and must, with a fine for every time either of you use the s***** or m*** words. As an added bonus the jar can be used to help fund your wedding chat free dates (see chapter six)

And for anyone who tells you that you should or must do something on your wedding day, leave them with this thought-provoking quote:

> *"The most damaging phrase...is "We've always done it this way!""* – Grace Hopper

Try not to use all or nothing thinking

It's easy to view things in absolutes, as black and white, rather than in the shades of grey they usually are. When Aunt Maybel massively over-reacts to the fish and chip van it's easy to move her from category one – the wonderful loving and supportive people in your life - to category two – people who strongly dislike, perhaps even hate, you for what would appear to be no valid reason. The truth is Aunt Maybel is a flawed individual who makes mistakes. Yes, she's acting out of order and treating you badly. She's putting her needs and wishes ahead of yours on your wedding day which isn't acceptable. But this doesn't make Aunt Maybel a bad person, she's simply acting badly.

I'm not suggesting you give in to Aunt Maybel's unreasonable complaints, but I am suggesting that you keep a balanced view of Aunt Maybel. If Aunt Maybel persists in her unfair demands – then it's perfectly ok to want to spend less time with her. There's no reason to feel guilty about feeling this way – it's normal behaviour. However, if Aunt Maybel behaves fairly and properly in other areas, perhaps for the sake of the relationship you can simply agree to disagree, like adults, regarding the fish and chip van.

Avoid the mental filter

The mental filter can cause us to minimise the positives and maximise the negatives – very dangerous mentally.

On a personal level, I experienced some challenging relatives during our wedding planning process. For some time this was all I was able to focus on, spending days crying about our situation. This meant I wasn't noticing the amazing things we were achieving in our wedding planning. My mental filter was maximising the negatives which meant I wasn't even noticing the positives. With time, amazing friends and advice, I was able to readjust my mental filter. I was able to see how massively the positives outweighed the negatives and start enjoying the wedding planning process once again.

In reality there are usually a lot more positives than negatives in any situation, they can just be harder to focus on at first. Aunt Maybel might be being a nightmare, but you may also have found an amazing dress, a delicious cake supplier, a banging venue and most importantly of all, you have found and are marrying the love of your life!

I recommend drawing up a list, by this point you've probably realised I love lists, with two columns:

Dealing With Difficult People

Negatives	Positives

Fill in this table with all the positive things going on in the wedding planning process and any negative things. I guarantee you the positive list will be longer than the negative one! Refer to and update the list whenever you feel overwhelmed and need to reset your mental filter.

Surround yourself with love and support

Lastly, I recommend surrounding yourself with love and support. Wedding planning is an amazing but intense process which is meant to be enjoyable. There is nothing wrong with minimising the time you spend around people who make you feel bad and you don't need to feel guilty about this basic self-preservation.

> **Top Tip**
>
> Talking things over can be hard at first – but it often really helps to know you are not alone. Remember to communicate with your partner too!

On the flip side, spend as much time as possible around people who are genuinely excited and enthusiastic about your wedding. Make sure these people know how much you appreciate them for the gems they are. Sometimes they aren't nearby, but the joys of modern technology means most are only a phone or a video call away. During the wedding planning process, I spoke to my mum most days, updating her about even the most minor things. This was amazing, she was genuinely excited to hear about everything - even the blue insoles I'd found for my shoes. For every negative person there is always at least one positive person who wants to be there for you! Try to focus on this.

Furthermore, utilise your partner's love and support. Remember you are a team and are planning this wedding together. If Aunt Maybel's behaviour is upsetting you, make sure you talk to one another about it and face it together. From personal experience, though it can be incredibly tough at the time, experiences like this can bring the two of you even closer together.

In summary, if you happen upon difficult people when planning your wedding please never feel alone, it's sad but true that most couples planning their wedding will experience this. The key is how you choose to deal with it and that it your choice entirely! I recommend using the things that are going well page to note down successes – look back at this when you feel everything is falling apart to remind yourself that this isn't the case.

How To Plan A Wedding Without Killing Anyone

Summary

- Weddings can bring out sides you haven't previously seen in people before –both good and bad.

- Try not to let one souring relationship affect the whole wedding planning process –it is up to you how you choose to deal with other people's challenging behaviour.

- Try not to over generalise – one person's opinion isn't everyone's.

- Avoid using the words should and must – this is <u>your</u> wedding day.

- Try not to use all or nothing thinking – things are rarely black and white.

- Avoid maximising negatives and minimising positives.

- Surround yourself with the love and support you both deserve and don't feel guilty shying away from those who are bringing you down.

Things that are going well

....
....
....
....
....
....
....
....
....
....
....
....
....
....
....
....
....
....
....
....
....
....
....
....

Chapter Twelve

The Bride's Outfit

There's a lot of pressure to look your best on your wedding day. In my opinion every bride looks beautiful as she exudes love and happiness. I've never been someone who's full of self-confidence. Like many of us, I often look in the mirror and am overly harsh on myself. That said, on my wedding day I felt beautiful – the way my now-husband looked at me made me feel like the most beautiful woman in the world. This wasn't something I had expected to feel. If only there had been a way to bottle this feeling for future use! You too will feel beautiful on your wedding day, enjoy this feeling.

This is your special day and a day that you definitely deserve to treat yourself – buy the dress you really want, wear the lingerie you want to wear, spoil yourself with jewellery that will always remind you of that special day.

The Bride's Outfit

Obviously, budget can be a limiting factor at times, but where there's a will, there's a way! Whether that's saving up a little extra for a particular dress or figuring out what it is you love about it and finding a more affordable version of this.

> **Top Tip**
>
> Shedding for the wedding is a great excuse to get fit – but go easy on yourself. Wedding planning can be stressful and not an easy time to lose large amounts of weight. Remember your partner loves you how you are!

The dress

Some of us will have dreamt of our wedding dress from a young age, have watched numerous episodes of "Say Yes to the Dress" and feel like we know exactly what we want in our dress. Others may feel very overwhelmed at the idea of spending so much money on a dress that we'll wear for just one day. There's no right way to feel about the wedding dress. So, accept how you feel and stop thinking about how you should feel.

When it comes to picking a wedding dress there are several main styles of dress:

- Ball-gown
- Princess
- Bateau
- A-line
- Modified A-line

- Mermaid
- Trumpet
- Column or Sheath
- Tea-length
- Mini

My recommendation would be to try different styles of dress – even if you are sure you want a specific style, you may surprise yourself by falling in love with another style. Try on many dresses, even after you think you've found the one; feel free to try on more if you'd like – why not! On top of the more general style there are different materials, different strap styles, different neckline styles and even different skirt styles. The choice can be overwhelming – but the good news is that there is definitely a dress out there for you!

When it comes to where to look for your dress there are also many options. These include:

- Smaller boutique stores
- Chain stores – these can vary significantly in price
- Charity shops
- High street stores
- Online

Each of these options has their own pros and cons. Smaller boutiques can be more personalised but can often (though not always) carrier a higher price tag. Be aware that many smaller boutique stores require appointments to be booked in advance and some may charge a fee per guest accompanying you.

The Bride's Outfit

Chain stores can be busier, less personalised and feel a little less special and more rushed. That said, they often have similar style dresses for a snip of the price compared to more boutique style stores. I myself found my dress at Wed2Be in Newcastle where the staff were lovely and patient. I bought my dream dress at a price we could afford and had a wonderful experience with my parents.

Charity shops often have second-hand dresses at more affordable prices with the added bonus that the cost of your dress will go to needy causes. Second-hand dresses can also be found online through Facebook and other sites specifically designed for selling second hand dresses. These are both great options for finding a dress you might love but be unable to afford at full retail price.

Some high street stores have recently brought out new bridal ranges with beautiful but affordable options. Some dresses are selling for less than £100; this can be a great option for those on a budget.

Stores selling wedding dresses include:

- Dorothy Perkins
- Topshop
- Misguided
- Coast
- Monsoon
- Phase Eight
- ASOS (online)
- Boohoo (online)

> "Cinderella never asked for a prince. She asked for a night off and a dress"
>
> -Kiera Cass

The Bride's Outfit

Online options offer a seemingly endless variety of style and budget options. For those on a tight budget and prepared to take a risk wedding dresses can be bought at very low prices from abroad. There are Facebook groups with seller reviews and real-life photos (such as China Wedding Dresses – Success Stories) – I would recommend visiting these before purchasing from an online seller so that you can make an informed choice.

> **Top Tip**
>
> Pick a new and/or special perfume and wear this in your wedding day. You can then associate this smell with your wedding day forever.

The veil

Some women choose to wear a veil, others don't - do what feels right for you. Veils can be expensive – costing hundreds of pounds. Do make sure your veil compliments your dress well by both on together. If you buy the dress and veil together at the same shop then this is an easy task. If not, make sure to try the veil on at a dress fitting to make sure you are happy.

Different lengths of veil, in length order, include:

- Blusher
- Shoulder length
- Elbow length

- Fingertip length
- Waltz length
- Chapel length
- Cathedral length

Veils can be bought at mostly the same options for dress buying. For those on a budget though I would recommend looking on eBay. My elbow-length veil was just £1.88. I had bought it on a whim, thinking it would be a laugh for my hen do, if nothing else. When it arrived, it was perfect and went beautifully with my dress. I couldn't believe my luck!

The lingerie

Once you've selected your dress, treat yourself to some good quality, comfortable but sexy lingerie for your wedding day. Make sure the lingerie works with your dress and gives you the lift and support you need. Good lingerie can make all the difference to how you feel – and you won't regret it on your wedding night!

> **Top Tip**
>
> Remember to bring your lingerie and shoes to dress fittings to allow the seamstress to fit the dress properly to how your shape and height will be on the day.

The shoes

Pick a pair of shoes that you love for your wedding day. I would recommend only wearing

The Bride's Outfit

shoes with a heel that you can walk comfortably in. You don't want to feel like Bambi walking down the aisle!

If you are wearing heels, I suggest having a second more comfortable pair of flats just in case your feet get tired and sore. Dancing into the night, the last thing you want holding you back is a pair of heels you can't dance properly in. These can also come in handy for any more demanding first dances.

I personally wore flats all day – if it's good enough for Wonder Woman, it's good enough for me! I'm quite tall so don't normally wear heels and wanted to be able to move around freely on my wedding day. Plus no one could even see my wonderfully jewelled and glittered shoes below my dress – a travesty if you ask me!

Whatever you choose to wear - remember to wear in your shoes before the big day to avoid blisters!

The jewellery

Pick out some nice jewellery that compliments your dress – earrings, necklace and bracelet(s). Wedding jewellery can easily be overlooked but when chosen well can finish off the bridal look perfectly.

> **Top Tip**
>
> Have your engagement ring cleaned before your big day – it will add an extra sparkle you didn't even know was possible.

As a bonus, this jewellery will be extra special as it will forever remind you of your big day! For those of us not confident in mixing and matching, an easy way to get complimenting jewellery is to buy a matching set.

Jewellery can also be your something borrowed if a friend or relative is willing and has a piece of sentimental value or even something you just really love.

The Bride's Outfit

<u>Summary</u>

- You are going to look amazing on your wedding day!

- There are many different styles of dress and options that can fit all budgets.

- Veils also come in a wide range of styles and prices.

- The right lingerie can make you feel like a million dollars.

- Pick shoes you can walk comfortably and make sure you have some dancing shoes!

- Don't forget to choose jewellery to finish your bridal look.

Bridal Outfit

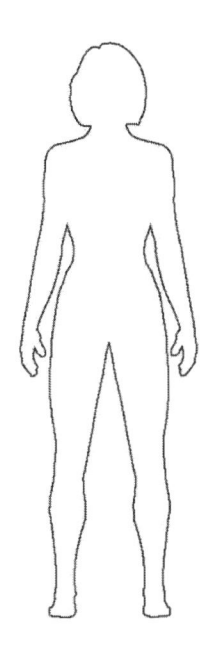

Veil:

Lingerie:

Shoes:

Jewellery:

Perfume:

Chapter Thirteen

Hair and Make-up

Good hair and make-up can make all the difference to your look and massively increase your confidence. My recommendation would be, if your budget allows, to invest in an expert. Nerves can make hands incredibly shaky, not ideal when trying to apply eyeliner on your big day! That and it feels incredible to have someone do your hair and make-up for you, and if not on your wedding day then when can you be pampered like this?

Hair

There are many factors that come into play when choosing your hair style, including:

- Your dress
- Your hair type
- Your hair length
- Accessories i.e. veil and/or hair pieces

Top Tip

Pinterest is perfect for browsing different hair and make-up styles – ideal for showing your hair stylist and make-up artist exactly what you want too!

How To Plan A Wedding Without Killing Anyone

- Your wedding theme

Whether to wear your hair up or down is usually your first decision. If your dress has an incredible back and your long hair would cover this, hair up is the more obvious choice. If you feel more comfortable with your hair down then go for this.

Hair type and length can be restrictive when it comes to selecting your wedding hair - try to work with, not against, your hair. My hair will simply not hold a curl, so long flowing curls was never an option for me. However, an up do with the illusion of curls was possible thanks to an amazing hair stylist, hours of work and lots of hair spray!

If you have a specific hair piece or veil in mind – try to visualise how this would work with your hairstyles. Similarly, if your wedding is themed – it might be worth considering how different styles would work with your theme.

When it comes to choosing a wedding hair style, I would recommend browsing through Pinterest and wedding magazines and saving ones you like. This is extremely enjoyable, though be careful of missing your stop on the train or bus! At first it may seem overwhelming as so many of them are absolutely stunning but you'll soon start to develop a preference for a general style.

I strongly advise booking a trial with your hair stylist at least 3-5 weeks before your big day. This gives you a chance

Hair and Make-up

to show them the styles you like, for them to try them with your hair and for you to see how it looks on you. This is also an opportunity to check out your hair stylist's work before the big day. Work with your stylist to make the look you want work for you.

> **Top Tip**
>
> Make sure you take your veil and/or any hair piece(s) to your hair trial for your hair stylist to work with.

Make-up

Similar to hair, I would recommend browsing through Pinterest to see what wedding make-up styles you like. My main recommendation for wedding make-up would be to choose a look that compliments your natural beauty rather than masking it. If you're unrecognisable walking down the aisle, it could cause all sorts of issues!

I'm no make-up expert, and was particularly nervous about my makeup as I have no idea what suits me and what doesn't. A professional make-up artist can take the looks you like and adapt them to work for you. My make-up artist introduced me to individual false lashes which were amazing – they were so subtle but made my lashes that little bit fuller and gave my eyes that extra pop. I would definitely recommend them for people who aren't sure about the more full-on look of false lashes.

I also recommend booking a trial 3-5 weeks before your wedding day. If you plan on wearing fake tan, do this before the trial to allow the makeup artist to work with the same complexion that they will be working with on the day.

Doing your own hair and make-up

If the budget won't allow for an expert, or you would simply prefer to do your own hair and/or make-up then my recommendation would be to practice your look as much as possible.

One thing to think about is the cost of the product: DIY hair and make-up can sometimes end up costing more than hiring a professional by the time you've purchased all the products and tools you require, so do bear this in mind.

Some people post photos of their attempts on Facebook wedding groups to get constructive feedback both from other brides and professionals. This advice can be invaluable and people are generally incredibly supportive on these groups.

"Makeup should never be used to hide yourself. It should be used to enhance your natural beauty"

~Kira Carl

Choosing a hair stylist and make-up artist

When choosing a hair stylist and make-up artist it is a good idea to look at reviews of their work, either online or by word of mouth if possible. Facebook groups are great for this, as is Google. I simply Googled hair and make-up artists in the area I was getting married and found a website I loved the feel of and the examples of their work. I checked out reviews then emailed the team and the rest, as they say, is history.

Some argue that it is best to have a separate hair stylist and make-up artist rather than a jack of all trades. I wouldn't say this is a hard and fast rule, as some people are genuinely great at both – check out their work to find out. Others may have a team consisting of hairstylist(s) and make-up artist(s).

If your bridal party also want their hair and/or make-up doing, let your hair stylist and make-up artist know as soon as possible. They will likely need more than one person if working with a larger group. Be wary of anyone who claims to be able to take on more work than seems possible. For my wedding we had two wonderful women who could do both hair and make-up working on myself and two of my bridesmaids.

My recommendation would be to book earlier for more popular dates and more rural areas where hair stylists and makeup artists may be harder to come by. Typically, people book them around 5-6 months before the big day – but if

Hair and Make-up

you know who you want then get in touch as soon as possible to find out their availability.

The run up to the wedding

Starting at least the month before the wedding, try to take good care of yourself and your skin. This is all stuff we would ideally be doing all the time, but life can often get in the way! This includes:

- Drinking plenty of water
- Eating healthily
- Sleeping enough
- Using lip balm daily
- Cleansing and removing make-up every evening
- Moisturising daily
- Exfoliating once a week
- Keeping your brows tidy

> **Top Tip**
>
> Ensure your beautiful blank canvas is well cared for – lipstick always looks nice applied to lips that aren't dry and chapped – and you'll feel better too!

If you intend to cut or colour your hair try to do it at least a week before your big day and avoid intense conditioning treatments in the week before the wedding.

Try to wash your hair the night before, rather than on the day and use only a little light conditioner on the ends of the hair. This will help make the hair less slippery and therefore able to hold curls and updos better.

On the day

Your hair stylist and make-up artist should be in touch before the big day with a time plan – especially if they are also doing your bridesmaids hair and/or make-up. I would recommend circulating this plan to your bridesmaids so they are aware of timings.

On the morning your make-up artist will want you make-up and product free – a beautiful blank canvas for their art. Be sure to wear a gown or button down top to get ready in. Once your hair and make-up are completed and you want to change into your dress, the last thing you want to do is drag a tight-necked T-shirt over it all!

> ## Top Tip
>
> Don't wear a bra on the morning of the wedding to avoid bra marks on your back and shoulders when you change into your dress.

Hair and Make-up

Summary

- Good hair and make-up can finish a look and massively increase your confidence.

- Select hair and makeup styles you like using Pinterest, magazines and Google.

- Work with a professional to make these looks work for you.

- Always look at reviews before selecting a professional.

- Look after yourself in the run up to the wedding.

- Wear a button-down shirt to get ready on the morning – treat yourself to a cute one!

Hair styles

Hair and Make-up

<u>Makeup styles</u>

Chapter Fourteen

The Groom's Outfit

It's not just the Bride who experiences the pressure to look her best on her wedding day. That said, as for the bride, every groom looks incredibly handsome when filled to the brim with love and happiness. Your wedding day is your opportunity to dress up – nothing is too much! Men who might usually never have occasion to wear a suit can go all-out. Others might choose to be a bit more casual and relaxed. There's no right or wrong answer, and whatever you wear, your partner is marrying you for you, not an outfit. When you and your partner's eyes meet, you will feel like the most handsome and luckiest man on the planet. Remember to enjoy this feeling.

> **Top Tip**
>
> As for the bride, shedding for the wedding is a great excuse to get fit – but go easy on yourself. Wedding planning can be stressful and not an easy time to lose large amounts of weight. Remember your partner loves you how you are!

The Groom's Outfit

It's important to remember that this is your special day too and though the focus can often be on the bride's dress; this is definitely a day that you deserve to treat yourself. Take someone special with you suit shopping, perhaps parents, the best man, groomsmen, a sibling and make a day of it. If it's good enough for the bride, then not the groom? It's also handy to have support and opinions – so remember to surround yourself with loving and constructive people. Choose carefully!

My husband decided that if he couldn't see my dress, I couldn't see his "outfit" as he kept referring to it. This was fair enough and actually made it more magical walking down the aisle as I saw him for the first time in his suit. He looked absolutely dashing!

Obviously, budget can be a limiting factor at times, but where there's a will, there's a way! Whether that's saving up a little extra for a particular suit, or renting instead of buying in order to stretch your budget a little further.

The suit

On their wedding day, the groom traditionally wears a suit. There's a vast array of choices with many different styles and colours. When it comes to picking a suit there are several main styles to choose from, ordered from most to least formal:

- White tie – tailcoat, waistcoat, bowtie, dress shirt, dress trousers, dress shoes and cufflinks
- Black tie – tuxedo jacket, bowtie, dress shirt, cummerbund, dress trousers, Oxford shoes and cufflinks
- Modern – suit, tie, formal shirt, belt, derby shoes and cufflinks
- Smart casual – smart jacket, casual shirt, chinos and brogues

Obviously, it's your day and your outfit, so feel free to mix and match between the styles and find whatever works for you. You can even go with something completely different that represents you and your roots and culture – a kilt perhaps!

> **Top Tip**
>
> An option to personalise your outfit and add a special touch is to design your own unique tie – you can even design ties for your Best man and groomsmen.

Things to consider when choosing a suit include:

- The venue – what style of suit works with the venue and theme. For example, if you're getting married on a tropical beach, more casual, lightweight and breathable material might be more appropriate
- The time of year and climate – for example a thick wool suit might work better for a December wedding than a mid-summer heatwave wedding

The Groom's Outfit

- Your own style – wear something you feel confident and comfortable in
- The wedding theme and style – top and tails might be more appropriate to a more high-brow occasion

More important than all of these considerations is your own personal choice. Choose a suit that makes you feel amazing, one that you can't wait to wear. If you feel great, you will exude confidence and will look great!

Of course, others may choose to dress more casually for a wedding. It's all about what works for you as a couple, so don't feel pressured to conform to societal norms. That said, it's important to be on the same page. If the bride is wearing a full-on ball gown and tiara, she might not appreciate you turning up in shorts and T-shirt.

Top Tip

When buttoning your suit, remember:

- One button suit
  – button when standing, unbutton when seated
- Two button suit
  – button <u>top only</u> when standing, unbutton when seated
- Three button suit
  – Top button optional, middle button always buttoned; lower button never buttoned

"Suit up!"

-Barney Stinson

The Groom's Outfit

The shoes

Pick a pair of shoes that you love for your wedding day. Dress shoes can seem complicated and full of jargon but what matters most is finding a pair of shoes you are excited to wear – that both look and feel good.

If you are particularly interested in understanding the jargon of Oxford or Balmoral (closed lacing) versus Derby or Blucher (open lacing) and semi brogue (cap-tope rather than wingtip) versus full brogue (wingtips) then feel free to research online. However, in my opinion this is entirely unnecessary – just go for what you think looks good.

It may seem obvious, but make sure your shoes go with the outfit you have chosen – both in terms of colour and style. If you're unsure then just ask people around you who will be more than happy to help.

Whatever you choose to wear - remember to wear in your shoes before the big day to avoid blisters!

How To Plan A Wedding Without Killing Anyone

Summary

- You are going to look incredibly handsome on your wedding day!

- Consider keeping your suit a surprise for the big day, as the bride does with her dress.

- There are many different styles and colours of suits and options that can fit all budgets.

- Pick shoes you can walk comfortably in and be sure to wear them in before the big day.

Groom's Outfit

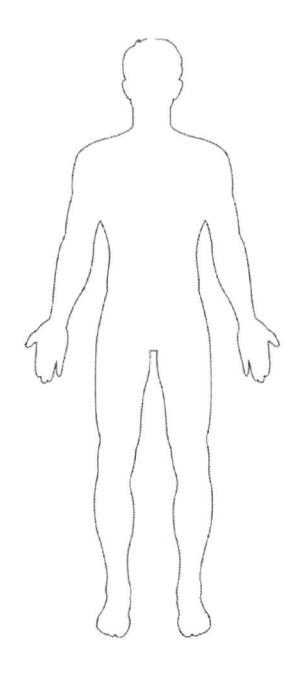

Jacket:

Shirt:

Tie or bowtie:

Trousers:

Shoes:

Other:

Chapter Fifteen

Bridal Party Outfits

As covered in chapter seven, the bridal party is the group of people you have chosen to fulfil the traditional wedding roles. The bridal party will expect you to communicate to them any expectations around what they should or shouldn't be wearing. In this chapter we will cover traditions and how best to approach each member of the bridal party's outfit. As usual, this is a guide and it's completely up to you how you approach this. Every wedding is unique and you as a couple know best what will work for your big day.

<u>Maid or matron of honour and bridesmaids</u>

Typically, the maid or matron of honour and bridesmaids will wear dresses – though some more modern weddings have seen them wearing and rocking suits or even other options. The group can all wear matching outfits, or the maid of honour can have a slightly different dress as to differentiate her. Another increasingly popular option is to have mis-matched dresses in different styles but the same or coordinating colours. This can look amazing – check out Pinterest to see what catches your eye. Think about how you want your photos to look and go with that.

Remember to think about the shapes and sizes of your bridesmaids. Beautiful women come in all shapes and sizes and it's important to appreciate that whilst a dress may look amazing on one particular shape and size, it might be a nightmare for someone with a different shape and size. A good example are dresses that require the wearer to go bra-less – whilst this may look amazing on your friend who is a 32C, this could be an absolute no-no for your friend who is a 36FF. The best way to deal with this is to talk to everyone. Better still, organise a girly shopping trip. This is a great opportunity to find out what styles work for everyone, at the same time as having fun and helping the group to bond. Who knows – you might even find the dress or dresses on your shopping trip!

> **Top Tip**
>
> A smart option can be to pick dresses that can be re-worn (sometimes with a bit of altering) after the wedding – this can soften the blow of the expense, but isn't for everyone.

In terms of shoes, accessories (bags and jewellery), hair and make-up – it is key to let everyone know what you expect. If you want all of the ladies with matching shoes then let them know. You might be able to buy them all together in such case. If you're happy for them to wear their own accessories as long as they are a certain colour, then let them know. If you want them all looking unique, again let them know. There's no right or wrong way here – just choose what works for you and your bridal party and communicate to them all clearly.

> **Top Tip**
>
> Stunning dresses can be ordered online for a lot cheaper than in most bridal stores. Check out FB pages for reviews and photos of actual dresses from different sellers.

Flower girl

Typically, the flower girl(s) will wear a cute dress. It's important to communicate with their parents and ensure they are happy and comfortable with what their child is wearing. Furthermore, make sure the child themselves is happy with the outfit. If she is over the moon and excited to be wearing her outfit, she is more likely to behave well and cooperate with her flower sprinkling duties than if she is uncomfortable, overheating and irritable.

"You're never fully dressed without a smile"

-Annie (Martin Charnin)

Best man and groomsmen

Typically, the best man and groomsmen will wear suits – though it really is up to you as a couple. The group will traditionally wear matching suits. It is important to consider what the groom is wearing when choosing attire for the groomsmen. If the groom is wearing smart casual for a beach wedding, the groomsmen might look a bit odd if they are all in white tie.

A shopping trip is a great opportunity to find out what styles look good on everyone and can be followed with a nice meal to help the group to bond pre-stag do. You might even find the right suit on your trip, ticking another item off the to-do list.

> **Top Tip**
>
> Suits can be rented rather than bought, an especially attractive option for suit styles that may only be worn on this one special occasion.

If you're on a tighter budget and aren't concerned about exact matches, simply ask the groomsmen to wear a black suit. Most men will already have a smart suit and be happy to just wear that. The look can then be personalised with different colour shirts, ties and so on.

In terms of shoes and accessories – as for the rest of the bridal party, it is key to let everyone know what you expect. If you want all of the men wearing matching shoes, or have any other outfit requirements, then let them know.

Bridal Party Outfits

Ring bearer

Typically, the ring bearer will wear a suit in-keeping with the groomsmen in terms of style and colour. As for the flower girl(s), it's important to communicate with parents and ensure they are happy and comfortable with what their child is wearing. Again, make sure the child themselves is happy with the outfit. If they are over the moon and excited to be wearing their outfit, they are more likely to behave well and cooperate.

Junior bridesmaids and groomsmen

Junior bridesmaids and groomsmen typically wear more age-appropriate versions of the attire chosen for the adult bridesmaids and groomsmen. As for the flower girl(s) and ring bearer, it is important to speak with the parents regarding expectations on both sides. Also speak with the child – they are likely incredibly excited to be a part of your big day, so feed off that excitement and enjoy the process of selecting an outfit alongside them.

Parents of the bride and groom

Whilst most couples allow their parents to choose their own attire, with a few guidelines here and there, some couples will go shopping with their parents to pick out their outfits with them. This can be a fun opportunity to spend time with parents before the wedding. Remember the wedding is a big deal for them too and they will likely be anxious to look their best but not too overdressed.

A key thing to bear is mind is that parents can be very nervous about how their outfit will compare to their in-law's outfits. They won't want to look too over- or under-dressed. A nice way around this can be a group shopping trip with a meal – if time and relative distances make this an option. Another option for more long-distance set-ups could be a WhatsApp group to discuss outfits and send photos.

Who should cover what?

In terms of who is paying for what, this can be an awkward conversation but an extremely important one. This can be quite a contentious topic on a lot of wedding forums – but there's no right or wrong way to do it. Every wedding has a different budget, and as long as your bridal party are ok with your decision then that's your business. If you are expecting them to pay, give them notice so that they can save enough to cover the cost. Another option is to pay for some parts, but not others – again here, communication is integral. Make sure everyone is on the same page.

Bridal Party Outfits

Summary

- Have a look at Pinterest to come up with ideas about how you would like your bridal party to look – there really are endless possibilities.

- A fun shopping trip (always with food!) can often help confusion and whip up excitement.

- Communication is key – talk to your bridal party about what they like and what they feel comfortable in, talk to them about how you envisage them looking, talk to them about who is paying for what. Things will go much more smoothly if everyone is clear and on the same page!

Bridal Party Outfits

Maid or matron of honour:

Bridesmaids:

Flower girl:

Best man:

Bridal Party Outfits

Groomsmen:

Ring bearer:

Junior bridesmaids and groomsmen:

Parents of the bride:

Parents of the groom:

Chapter Sixteen

The Hen and Stag Do

The hen and stag do often seem to be referred to as a "last night of freedom" or "final fling before the ring". Whilst this is all often said in jest, it is a good excuse for a pre-wedding day and night out with your closest friends and sometimes family ahead of your upcoming nuptials. Hen and stag dos are often expected to be big boozy nights out with hilarious shenanigans and often risqué activities, but it's important to remember that the event should be one you enjoy, not one you feel you must attend.

Typically, the hen do will be organised by the hen's bridal party, headed up by her maid of honour, and the stag by the groomsmen, headed up by the best man. If you feel more comfortable planning the event, then let your friends know and do this. There

---

Top Tip

Sten dos- joint hen and stag dos are becoming an increasingly popular alternative to separate hen and stags.

can also be a spectrum of involvement – my best friend was keen for me to plan the weekend but to let her look at the plans and check she was happy with it all. Find what works for you and your friends and make sure to communicate with one another.

The first key decision, after who will plan the event, is who will attend the event. It's up to you whether you feel more comfortable with larger groups of people or prefer a more intimate group. Some people choose just to invite close friends, other choose to invite their family and future in-laws to be. Others choose to invite different people to different parts – for example friends and family to the afternoon activity and dinner, then just friends for the evening activity.

> **Top Tip**
>
> Don't feel pressured to invite a massive group of people – sometimes the smallest gatherings are the most intimate and memorable. Equally if a large group is what you want – go for it!

In terms of activities, the possibilities are endless. Though there's nothing wrong with a boozy night out, alternative options include:

- Escape room
- Musical or play show
- Treasure Hunt

How To Plan A Wedding Without Killing Anyone

- Clay pigeon shooting or archery
- Weekend away – maybe even abroad
- Zorbing
- Karaoke
- Festival
- Wine tasting
- Theme Park
- Afternoon tea or a special meal
- Murder mystery
- Spa day

The key is to find something you enjoy – don't be afraid to communicate this to whoever is organising the event. That said, do bear in mind your guests – just because you enjoy fire-eating upside down after hiking up Mount Everest, it doesn't mean they will. Try to find an activity you love that everyone involved will find some joy in – or at least be able to feign enjoyment.

> **Top Tip**
>
> Be clear on what you are comfortable with – if you don't want a stripper then make sure the organiser knows this. They won't want to make you upset or uncomfortable, so help them out.

> "Good friends don't let you do stupid things alone"
> -unknown

A good option for any downtime can be games – this can also help bring the group together if they don't already know one another well, or if there are multiple separate friendship groups. A quick google of hen/stag do games will bring up numerous options along with how to play them.

For weekends away and/or more expensive hen/stag dos – it's a good idea to discuss cost with guests before booking and setting your heart on any one thing. The hen/stag may have to prioritise the guest list versus the cost – in that the more expensive the trip, the fewer people may be able to attend. Whilst there is no right or wrong priority – it's important to make the decision that works for you here. By providing the guests with a rough idea of costs, you'll get a good idea of who would come.

This is also a good time to discuss dates too – a much less awkward topic! A doodle poll can be a good idea to find a date that works for the majority, if not everyone. Though traditionally hen/stag dos have taken place the night before the wedding, it's a good idea to hold it at least a few weeks in advance to give plenty of time for any recovery required. It can also be a nice idea to have the hen and stag do at the same time, where possible, so neither partner is sat home alone experiencing FOMO, wondering what the other is getting up to. I've never had any trust

> **Top Tip**
>
> Email whoever is organising the hen/stag do a list of guests along with their contact details to make it easier for them to send out invites.

The Hen and Stag Do

issues with my husband, but being sat home alone for the weekend while he jetted off for his stag do wasn't the most enjoyable experience.

Once who, what and when have been decided, it's time to send the invites out. The invites to hen/stag dos can be as formal or as informal as you prefer. Some choose to create beautiful hand-crafted ones; others use their computers and some just text or call guests. The most important thing is that all the guests know where and when they need to be, far enough in advance to organise this. If you need guests to bring anything this is a good time to communicate that too.

The finishing touches can make a hen/stag do – from confetti to balloons, check out your local bargain shops for affordable hen/stag décor. Make sure to check out Pinterest for ideas. Another idea is to have a dress code – whether that's colourful and fun, suave and sophisticated or even fancy dress! On one of my close friend's hen do, all the guests wore black and the bride wore white for our evening meal – the photos looked amazing.

On the day remember to relax and enjoy your hen/stag do – it is all just a bit of fun so let go and embrace that fun and you'll have an amazing time with your nearest and dearest.

How To Plan A Wedding Without Killing Anyone

Summary

- The hen/stag is traditionally organised by your bridal parties – but nowadays it's up to you how involved you want to be. Some like to plan their own, other people want complete surprises – do what works for you!

- First decide who will attend the event – try not to feel pressured to invite your entire wedding guest list. Invite who you want to celebrate with.

- Pick activities that you enjoy – this occasion is a celebration of you – but do consider the attendees too.

- Always consider dates and costs – this may affect who can make it and so may affect key decisions.

- Remember to relax and enjoy yourself!

Hen do

Guest list

Name   *Contact details*

Dates..

Budget..

                             Estimated cost

Transport
Food and drink
Accommodation
Activities
Other

Activities..
....
....

Accommodation...

Stag do

Guest list

Name	Contact details

Dates..

Budget..

	Estimated cost
Transport	
Food and drink	
Accommodation	
Activities	
Other	

Activities..
....
....

Accommodation..

158

Chapter Seventeen

Photography and Videography

You'll hopefully want to remember your wedding day forever and photography and videography is the way to do just that. From the look in your eyes as they meet your partner's walking down the aisle to the sheer delight of your family and friends as they celebrate into the night with you, detailed memories often fade over time. It's the responsibility of your wedding photographer and videographer to capture every little detail, so you can look back on their work and remember your special day.

Photography and videography can seem expensive, but it often rings true that you get what you pay for. Paying for quality and someone you can trust is priceless. That said, you could pay through the roof for a photographer only to find you hate their photography style, so research is key here. This chapter will explore how to find your ideal wedding photographer and videographer, so that you can choose the perfect fit for you as a couple.

Photography

Prior to searching for a photographer, it's useful to consider what style of photography you like. If you're anything like me, the technical terms mean nothing, so set aside some time to go through this list and research them, making notes about what you like and don't like.

> **Top Tip**
>
> Try to allocate a significant proportion of your wedding budget to photography and videography - many recommend at least 10%.

I've provided a brief explanation for each one, but as they say, a picture says a thousand words, and never has this been truer than here:

- Traditional – classic and often posed
- Photojournalistic – more informal, less posed, trying to report the day as it happens
- Black and white – quite self-explanatory really…
- Illustrative – emphasis is often more on the lighting, composition and background
- Portrait – more formal, directed and posed
- Natural – using natural light, often mixed with other styles

Photography and Videography

- Vintage – using colour distortion filters to add a rustic theme
- Fine Art – creative framing, lighting and composition with post-production editing
- Fashion – like modelling, creatively posed shots

Typically, a wedding photographer will mix styles - for example it's very common to ask for a photojournalistic approach but with some more traditional directed poses and a portrait session following the ceremony. Often the couple and family portraits are the ones the couple and their family choose to frame and display in their home, so do bear this in mind. Once you've decided on styles, search for a wedding photographer who works that way.

If you find yourself getting confused and hung up on all these technical terms, an easy way to find a photography style you like is to simply look through portfolios online or at wedding fairs. This is the easiest way to find a photographer you like, as you can simply pick what you love. Be sure to check out their online reviews too!

> **Top Tip**
>
> Photographs and videos, along with the rings, are often the only tangibles left after the wedding day, so it's important to ensure they at least meet your expectations.

Take a look at the different packages different photographers offer and their price lists. A package will typically include:

- Pre-wedding consultation
- Engagement shoot
- Specified number of hours' work on the day
- Specified number of high-resolution, fully-edited digital images from the day (typically 300-500 photos for a full 9-hour day)
- Personal use copyright license
- Professional photo album or book

Don't be afraid to talk to wedding photographers about personalising packages, for example you might prefer to make your own album or book (Wowcher often has deals on these – though do bear in mind it can be time consuming to do so) or not have an engagement shoot. We asked our photographer to add on an extra hour or two's coverage on the day in lieu of an engagement shoot and he was more than happy to do so.

When you find a wedding photographer you like – message them or call them. Get a feel for how they approach answering your questions. If you have met them at a wedding fair, even better. It's crucial that you get on well with your wedding photographer and that you feel at ease around them. They are going to be there by your side pretty much the entire day, capturing every special moment, so you want someone that will make this a pleasure not an ordeal. The ideal wedding photographer can fade into the background throughout the day but come forward and help you pose, when needed, in a manner that leaves you feeling comfortable and relaxed. Talk to as many as you need to online or over the phone to get a feel for them. I would recommend meeting in person, even just for a coffee, to discuss their style and your requirements for your special day. Meeting in person will make it much easier to decide if the photographer is suited to you as a couple – always follow your intuition here.

I was quite nervous, as I hate having my photograph taken and would never ordinarily pay for a person to follow me round with a camera!? The whole concept seemed quite alien! I obviously wanted memories of the day so put these feeling aside and am so happy I did. Our wedding photographer was so friendly and knew exactly how to help us relax and be ourselves in front of the camera. From the moment we met him, we knew he was perfect for our special day. I felt confident leaving the task in his hands and felt comfortable with him behind the camera, directing us when required and taking candid shots throughout the rest of the day. I must admit, despite usually hating photos of myself, I look back on our wedding photos and even I think I look beautiful!

> **Top Tip**
>
> A drone can be a cool way to get a big group shot of all the wedding guests – ask your photographer to see if they can do so.

Many photographers offer an engagement shoot which can be a good opportunity to test their style and your compatibility, as well as a chance to get some lovely photos of you as a couple. These photos can be used for your wedding invites too, should you want to. Don't be afraid to seize this opportunity to engage with your wedding photographer – let them know what you like or don't like, how you envisage them taking part in your special day and any other important details. And should the worst happen, and you don't get along well on the engagement shoot, don't be afraid to find a new wedding photographer!

As with any wedding supplier, I would recommend always signing a contract. Make sure you have the following key details in writing:

- Full names and contact information
- Details of your day
- Photography package details with an agreed rough number of photos
- Agreed post-production timescales
- Costs, payment terms and deposit required
- Client cancellation terms and refunds
- Photographer cancellation terms and refunds
- Contingency plans for last-minute illness of the photographer
- Details of copyright and reproduction
- Signatures

Photography and Videography

Though the photographer is the expert, and it's often best to leave the expert to it throughout the day, I would suggest providing a shot list of must-have photos. This way you can be confident that the photographs which are particularly important to you will not be missed. I would recommend a separate shot list (your jewellery, the bouquets and so on) and portrait list, and have provided my two lists as examples, though please do personalise them should you choose to use them (presumably you won't have exactly the same invite list as me, so the portrait list may be missing some relatives or have additional ones):

> **Top Tip**
>
> It's good etiquette to offer your photographer and videographer food – they can't be expected to work a full day with no food or breaks!

Shot list

- Bride getting ready
    - Mother and bride
    - Bride and bridesmaids
    - Bride and maid of honour
    - Dress reveal
    - Hairstyle close-up
    - Wedding dress
    - Bouquet

How To Plan A Wedding Without Killing Anyone

  - Full photo of bride in dress
  - Jewellery and perfume

- Groom

  - Full photo of groom in suit
  - Groom and groomsmen
  - Groom and best man
  - Ties, cufflinks, other accessories

- Rings

- Rooms decorated, especially aisle when room empty

- Groom waiting at altar

- Entrances down aisle

- Father seeing daughter for first time - reveal

- Grooms reaction and bridal entrance

- Vows

- Ring exchange

- First kiss (with guests behind?)

- Recession

- Confetti photos and receiving line

- Dinner photos

Photography and Videography

- Speeches
- Sparkler photos
- Wedding cake before cutting
- Bride and groom cutting cake
- First dance
- Father daughter dance

<u>Formal Portrait Session</u>

1. All guests
2. Bride and groom with all family
3. Bride and groom with grandparents, parents and siblings
4. Bride and groom with grandparents
5. Bride and groom with all parents
6. Bride with her parents
7. Bride and groom with parents and siblings of Bride
8. Bride and groom with parents and siblings of Groom
9. Groom with his parents
10. Groom with siblings

11. Bride and groom with all siblings

12. Bride and groom with siblings

13. Bride with siblings

14. Bride and groom with siblings

15. Bride and groom with Bride's aunt, uncle and cousins

16. Bride and groom with groom's aunt and uncle

17. Bride and groom with groom's cousins

18. Bride and groom with groom's cousins

19. Bride and groom with bridal party

20. Bride and groom with bridesmaids

21. Bride and groom with groomsmen

This list, especially the shot list, might be teaching your grandma to suck eggs a little bit for a professional wedding photographer. However, I would argue that it's better to be safe and sorry and ensure you have communicated exactly what you want – especially when it comes to the more individualised photos. For example, we gave our photographer specific instructions to photograph the ties that my husband had lovingly designed himself. For many couples, having photographs of the ties specifically might seem a little strange, but for us it was important.

Photography and Videography

The portrait list can also be incredibly useful when it comes to organisation – who needs to be where and when. Think through the order of the photographs to minimise the time spent switching people around – this will make the portrait session much quicker and less stressful!

> **Top Tip**
>
> Take the larger group photos first (all guests, all family and so on) then gradually "dismiss" guests – it's much easier than trying to get everyone back in one place – there's always someone at the loo!

"Photography is the beauty of life captured"

-unknown

Photography and Videography

Videography

It's a big worry for engaged couples that they may make a decision regarding their wedding day that they might later regret. This is never truer than the decision as to whether or not to hire a wedding videographer. A question I've seen asked numerous times in various wedding planning Facebook groups is "Did you have a wedding videographer? If not, did you regret it?". I would highly recommend getting a videographer, if you can afford it – but not at the expense of the photographer. Better to have good quality photos and no video than poor quality photographs and videos.

When it comes to choosing a videographer, the principles are basically the same as for the photographer, so I won't bore you by going back through it all in detail. Find a videographer whose style you like, who has great reviews and who you feel comfortable working with. Ideally meet with them, or at least video call with them before the big day.

> **Top Tip**
>
> A riskier but cost-saving option can be to hire a photography student to shoot your day, or someone looking to build their portfolio. Minimise risk by having a test shoot or engagement shoot first to ensure you like their work.

Many professional videographers will use both static and handheld cameras to capture a variety of shots and may want to visit the venue ahead of the day, to plan where best to place different cameras. Do your best to accommodate this, as knowing the venue layout will help them do a better job, from which you will ultimately benefit with a better-quality wedding video.

I would suggest putting your photographer and videographer in touch with one another before the day itself. They will have to work together, ensuring that they don't get in the way of one another's shots and may prefer to plan this in advance. This is especially important in smaller venues and rooms with tighter spaces that may be trickier to manoeuvre in.

Photography and Videography

<u>Summary</u>

- Photography and videography are incredibly important as they will capture memories and help them to last a lifetime.

- Make sure you allocate budget accordingly – this isn't the area to cut back on!

- Choose a photographer and videographer whose style and photos you like, who is reviewed positively and who you both get on well with.

- Set out a clear contract so that both parties know what is expected.

- Provide both with a list of must have shots and portraits so no key photos get missed – they aren't mind readers after all!

- Make sure your photographer and videographer have spoken in advance to agree how they will work alongside one another.

Photo must-shoots

SHOTS	PORTRAITS

Chapter Eighteen

The Ceremony

The ceremony can often be overlooked in terms of planning, even though it is the central part of the day, given a wedding is defined as the marriage ceremony along with accompanying celebrations.

I'm going to go back to basics here and explain the wedding ceremony step-by-step. Unless you've been to numerous weddings, the ceremony and its components can seem like a bit of a mystery and it's hard to personalise a process you don't really understand.

> **Top Tip**
>
> Unplugged ceremonies, where guests are asked to not take any photos, are becoming ever more popular – make sure to let guests know if this is what you want.

1. The processional

This is the grand entrance. It's completely up to you how you choose to do this. The big question is often whether the bride goes first (followed by her bridesmaids) or the bridesmaids go first (followed by the bride). There are advantages to both options, if the bride walks first it can be more dramatic and give the groom a better view of his bride. Furthermore, having your bridesmaids behind you means they can keep the train of your dress and veil looking perfect, making any necessary last-minute adjustments. On the other hand, with the bridesmaids first, it can be a wonderful announcement of your imminent arrival and gives them the chance to watch you walk down the aisle too. For the more nervous brides it can also make the experience less daunting.

> **Top Tip**
>
> One option is to have your bridesmaid walk down the aisle ahead of you, then leave a slight pause or change of music to give you your own defined entrance.

Another big question is who, if anyone, will walk you down the aisle. Traditionally the father of the bride walks her down the aisle but this is your big moment and you should do what feels right for you. Many women choose other options such as walking themselves down the aisle, having their mother walk them or other father-figures. At a friend's wedding recently, the two brides walked half-way down the aisle with their fathers then came together and the two brides walked one another down the aisle. This was truly beautiful!

Some processionals, often at larger weddings, are even bigger and can include (traditionally in the following order) the officiant, the groom, the best man, the bridesmaids and groomsmen (side by side), the maid of honour, the flower girl and ring bearer then the bride and her father alongside one another.

You will be asked to pick out at least one song for the processional. You can go for a more traditional option like "Canon in D" (J. Pachelbel) or the "The Bridal Chorus" from Lohengrin (R. Wagner), or you can choose a song that means something to you as a couple. It is worth putting a lot thought together into this decision, as this song will hold a special place in your heart following the wedding.

> **Top Tip**
>
> For a classy version of a modern song, you could find an instrumental version – piano or string versions work especially well.

2. Words of welcome and opening remarks

Once the processional is complete and everyone is in place, the officiant will usually say a few words of welcome and thank everyone for coming. The officiant will typically have a standard script they follow, but if you have anything you would like to include then check with them if they can do so. The officiant will then usually address you, as the couple about to be married, and talk about the importance of the vows you are about to make. Again, the officiant will often have a typical script, so do let them know if there is anything you would particularly like to include. For example, at a recent wedding I attended, the officiant spoke, at the couple's request, about how quickly a wedding day could pass by. She asked everyone in the room who was already married to remember their own wedding days and then asked that everyone take a moment to reflect on the love in that room, there and then. It was a really special moment.

3. Exchange of vows

You can choose to follow the classic and timeless ""to have and to hold, for better or for worse" vows or you can choose to write your own. Make sure you decide together which option you prefer and leave plenty of time to write them before the big day. There's

> **Top Tip**
>
> Make sure someone has a spare copy of your vows if you choose to write your own but haven't memorised them!

lot of guidance available from Uncle Google on writing vows (a topic that could warrant a book in itself) but what's most important is to make them personal to you as a couple.

4. Exchange of rings

This is pretty self-explanatory. Usually the best man hands the couple the rings – quite often the ring bearer is a child so is only entrusted with decorative rings. The couple then exchanges rings as the officiant instructs them to do so.

The bride will often wear her engagement ring on her other hand during the ceremony, as it can be quite fiddly and look clumsy taking it off under pressure, in order to put the wedding ring on.

"Love is friendship set on fire"

-Jeremy Taylor

5. Pronouncement of marriage and first kiss

Again, pretty self-explanatory – the "I now pronounce you husband and wife". Some officiants may still say man and wife so be sure to let them know if you have a preference.

6. Signing of the register

At this point the Bride and Groom will sign the wedding register alongside their two witnesses. These witnesses can be whoever you choose – often people will choose one person from either side of the family or wedding party – for example the mothers or the best man and maid of honour.

You will usually be asked to choose two or three songs to play as background music while the register is being signed. This is a great opportunity to personalise the ceremony by picking songs special to you as a couple.

7. Closing remarks

The officiant will now bring the ceremony to a close. Though they will usually have a standard script here, as throughout the ceremony, do let them know if there's anything specific you would like them to say.

8. The recessional

This is basically the reverse of the processional – the newly married couple exit first, followed by the wedding party and then the rest of the wedding guests.

Typically, music will be played, as for the processional. Here you can go traditional with a nice classical piece or pick a

The Ceremony

song that means something you to you both. Often couples go for something a bit more fun and upbeat for the recessional, to signal that the serious part is completed and the party about to start.

Readings

Throughout the ceremony you can add personalised readings at different points – check with your officiant as to where they allow readings in their ceremony formats. Readings are typically done by family members or close friends and are an excellent way to personalise the ceremony and include special people in your day. It may seem obvious, but make sure the people doing the readings are comfortable and happy to do so and perhaps consider whether or not they will do the reading well before choosing them.

There are so many options for wedding readings, though there are a select few more popular passages that you will probably hear read at several weddings throughout your life. Choose readings that work for you – don't shy away from the more popular pieces – after all they are popular for a reason! That said, the readings are a great opportunity to personalise the ceremony so feel empowered to pick ones that feel right for you as a couple.

> Top Tip
>
> Following the recessional is an excellent time to organise five minutes alone with your new husband or wife. It can be difficult to get precious time alone on your wedding day so seize this opportunity!

Do make sure your readings are a reasonable length – no one is expecting just a haiku, that said, making them sit through War and Peace will likely put a dampener on the day. As a rough guide – I would suggest nothing that takes longer than 3-5 minutes to read aloud.

The Ceremony

Summary

- The ceremony is the central part of your day and important not to overlook in terms of planning.

- Key components include:
    - The processional
    - Words of welcome and opening remarks
    - Exchange of vows
    - Exchange of rings
    - Pronouncement of marriage and first kiss
    - Signing of the register
    - Closing remarks
    - The recessional
    - Readings

- There are opportunities to personalise the ceremony throughout from the readings and scripts to the music – don't be afraid to make the ceremony a reflection of you as a couple.

Wedding Music

Music

The processional

....

Signing of the register

....

The recessional

....

Witnesses

....

....

Readings

....

....

....

....

....

Chapter Nineteen

Transport

In terms of transport for the big day, there are two main areas to think about – transport for the bridal party (including yourselves) and transport for the guests. Transport can initially seem like a small task, but getting everyone to the right place at the right time is integral to ensuring your day runs smoothly. It is therefore essential to book a service you can rely on, on the day. Furthermore, the style of the transport can really add to the theme of the day and make for amazing photos, so I encourage you to consider your choices carefully. This chapter will discuss wedding party and guest transport separately, as often the former is more extravagant than the latter.

Wedding Party

The first consideration when it comes to choosing transport is if and when you are going to need it. If everyone is staying at your venue the night before, getting ready at the venue and then staying for the ceremony, reception and the night of the wedding, then you obviously don't need wedding transport for yourselves or the bridal party. That said, if you would like to hire transport just for photos or would like to go for a ride around the block first, then go for it!

Most commonly wedding transport for you and the bridal party is required for some of the following:

- From where you are getting ready to the ceremony
- From the ceremony to the reception
- From the reception to where you are staying the night following the wedding

Once you know when you need the transport, you can look at your transport options and align them with your budget. Though most people book traditional wedding cars, which can be found online, there are other options to consider including:

- Horse and carriage
- Tractor
- Taxi
- Bike
- Horseback
- Bus
- Helicopter
- Walking

> **Top Tip**
>
> Friends and family with nice cars can provide a more budget-friendly option for wedding party transport.

Transport

Some of the options on this list might seem a bit crazy but remember it's your big day so pick what works for you! Extra quirkiness points if you can think of something not on this list. And remember there is no shame in a friend or family member driving you – if you pick the right person you can have extra reliability here too. I would encourage you to think through what fits with your theme, what kind of entrance you want to make and what you would like in your photos. If you're a shy groom or bride, turning up in a horse and carriage or landing in a helicopter might not be the low-key, no-pressure entrance you were hoping for. Equally if you want all eyes on you, they might be ideal. The beauty of wedding planning is there is no right or wrong choice – it depends entirely on what works best for you as a couple.

When you've decided on a mode of transport, take the time to look through the vendors in your local area. As with all wedding vendors, speak to friends and family, read reviews online and talk to the company themselves too to get a feel for which vendors you like and don't like. Always choose a

"Don't sit in the passenger seat, take the wheel"

-unknown

Transport

transport company you can trust to be on time – you do not want the stress of running late or waiting for the cars on our big day!

Once booked, make sure to let your photographer and videographer know the plan and whether or not you want photos enroute. Those special moments in the back of a car (please replace with whatever mode of transport you choose here) are often beautiful and treasured moments – you may want to capture them or you may prefer to have privacy, but do let the photographer and videographer know.

Wedding Guests

When it comes to your wedding guests, many couples choose to let guests make their own way to and from venues. All guests need is the address of the locations they need to be at and the relevant times, usually provided on their invites. If your venue can be hard to find, I would recommend putting up a little signage or leaving clear instructions as appropriate. Some people choose to put up signs in the style of road signs but personalised with their names and wedding date – this can be super practical and look very

> **Top Tip**
>
> Getting married at a hotel venue gives the option of everything happening in one place -this can not only be more cost effective but also help reduce the on the day stress of moving from place to place.

189

professional and classy too. Equally a nice large board sign can work well. I would recommend having a friend try to find the place ahead of the wedding, as a sort of trial run, just to flag up any issues other guests might face. You could also ask the venue for any common issues. This way you hopefully won't be dealing with any lost guests on the day.

Some couples may choose to provide transport for the guests – particularly if guests are coming from abroad. It can be a nice touch to organise a minibus to pick up guests from the airport, especially if they are all arriving on the same or similar flights, and shuttle them to their accommodation. Though this is definitely above and beyond, it will be very much appreciated by guests who may be a bit unsure of how to sort transport in a foreign country.

> **Top Tip**
>
> Make sure your photographer, videographer and any other vendors are able to get from one venue to another if the ceremony and reception are in different locations.

Other couples who have the ceremony and reception split across different venues, may choose to hire a bus to transport wedding guests between the two. Some couples may also choose to organise guest transport to and from accommodation. There are some beautifully decorated buses available so you can incorporate it as part of the guest experience.

Transport

All of this guest transport is very much above and beyond. Though it will likely be very much appreciated by guests, when I receive a wedding invite, I usually assume it will be my responsibility to get myself to and from the venue or venues. If your budget doesn't stretch to this degree of guest VIP treatment or you would simply rather spend the money you do have elsewhere, that's more than okay! Even if Aunt Mabel is telling you you're an embarrassment because you haven't shuttled her entire extended family and friends from around the world to the ceremony room but have instead just given them an address to come to, she's wrong! No sane person, or anyone who remembers the stress or expense of planning their own wedding, expects the couple to arrange and pay for the guest's transport!

In summary, when it comes to transport, the priority is reliability (and most often affordability). That said, it is an excellent area to personalise the wedding to your own taste. As I've said so often, choose what works for you.

Summary

- First consider if and when transport will be necessary on the day.

- Think about how you would like to travel, keeping your budget in mind.

- Choose a reliable and positively reviewed transport provider.

- Don't forget to consider wedding guest transport – and remember to communicate with them whether or not you will be providing it.

Wedding Transport

Getting ready location → Ceremony location

....
....
....

Ceremony location → Reception location

....
....
....

Reception location → Accommodation

....
....
....

Chapter Twenty

Decoration

This chapter is really close to my heart, as I would class wedding décor as my favourite part of wedding planning, bar maybe the cake tasting. Wedding décor is often what sets your wedding aside, as it creates the general feeling and atmosphere that guests are greeted by upon arrival. They say first impressions count, and it is your general décor that will create this impression. Added to this, when it comes to your memories, your décor will be both the frame and backdrop through which you remember the day. In summary, wedding décor is important – so don't overlook it.

That said, wedding décor rarely goes wrong, as it is so personal and unique to every individual couple. Start by picking your theme and wedding colours. The moment I got engaged, I was bombarded with questions around the wedding theme – and I was perplexed as to what this question even meant. I just wanted a beautiful wedding, not a fancy dress Frozen or Toy Story themed party. Not that there's anything wrong with these, and some people do choose to have such themed weddings, it just wasn't what I

Decoration

wanted. I now understand that when it comes to weddings, themes are often a much more general idea used to convey the feeling you are aiming for with your wedding. For example:

- Bohemian
- Classic
- Country
- Glamorous
- Modern and contemporary
- Natural or woodland
- Retro
- Romantic
- Rustic
- Vintage

Pick one or even a complementary two or three of the above themes that speak to you as a couple and create a mood board of ideas and colours that you would like to incorporate for your wedding. Pinterest is ideal for this – I promise this book isn't sponsored by the platform, though you might assume so given the number of times I've mentioned it.

> **Top Tip**
>
> Décor is an easy area to get friends and family involved – have your mum make the bunting she enjoys making or your sister in law make the paper flowers you love – this can save money and also help friends and family feel involved. If you opt for this, please be realistic over what to expect unless your relatives are professionals.

With colours, I would recommend picking these alongside your theme, as the two often go hand in hand. Be sure to look at colour palettes to assess how well your colours go together. There are many "rules" around seasons and appropriate colour palettes – I say go with what's right for you both. There's nothing wrong with icy blues, or Christmassy reds and greens in summer or more floral or bright colours in winter. Do bear in mind seasonal stocking though, as it might be harder to find certain colours in store at certain times of year, if you're intending to look in more general stores for décor or clothing.

> **Top Tip**
>
> Check out other brides' DIY projects on Pinterest and various wedding planning Facebook groups.

Once you have a general idea of the décor theme and colours, it's time to think about what you want more specifically. I would recommend checking with your venue what is actually included in terms of décor. When we viewed our venue there had just been a wedding, and we fell in love with the beautiful white curtain backdrop in the ceremony room – it had fairy lights running vertically which made it look absolutely magical! When we sat down to discuss décor with our venue it emerged this wasn't included and, to our horror, was several hundred pounds extra should we wish to have it. Thankfully our venue was really understanding and were able to agree a discount on this – but it was a good lesson in being clear around what's included in what you are paying for. Once you know what the venue offers, it's your turn to be clear with them regarding what you want – make sure this is all written down so there are no misunderstandings or mistakes.

Once you are clear regarding what the venue is providing and what is up to you as a couple, it's a good idea to

Decoration

brainstorm ideas together. Definitely scroll through Pinterest or other sources of wedding photographs to get your creative juices flowing. I found it useful to think of each room individually.

Though the possibilities are endless, I'll provide an example list firstly for the ceremony room:

- Welcome sign
- Chairs and décor
- Signage – for example if it's an unplugged ceremony, or which side to sit
- Reserved seating signage for family and bridal party members
- Order of ceremony
- Registrar table décor
- Aisle runner
- Ceremony backdrop
- Confetti cones or baskets

Secondly for the wedding breakfast:

- Seating chart (if you have a seating plan) frame or stand
- Table and chair covers for the meal
- Centrepieces
- Top table décor
- Table numbers or names
- Plates, glasses and silverware
- Printed menus

And lastly for the reception:

- Table covers and décor for every table and activity

How To Plan A Wedding Without Killing Anyone

- Cake table décor
- Signage – for example explaining the guestbook, gift table or the favours
- Guestbook
- Dance floor décor
- Photo booth and props
- General wall décor – balloons, flowers or drapes
- Bathroom signage and bathroom baskets

Though obviously you likely won't need all of the above, the lists are just to give you a general idea – a sort of starting point from which to decide what you need. A nice touch can also be to provide for guests' practical needs according to the season – so perhaps on top of the bathroom baskets, some umbrellas, blankets, flip-flops, as appropriate.

> **Top Tip**
>
> Think practically when it comes to signage, what have you as a guest wanted to know at other weddings you've attended – for example, for me an order of the day is important.

Once you have a rough idea of what you need, it's time to decide who will provide what. You can choose to either DIY, rent or hire a professional to sort it for you. Most people will do a mixture of these options – do what works best for you. I would say though, that although DIY might seem at first glance like the cheapest option, it often isn't. This is especially true for more complex pieces that may

> **Top Tip**
>
> Be realistic with time frames when it comes to DIY-ing – wedding planning should be enjoyable so don't pile too much pressure on in terms of how much stuff you need to get done.

"Believe in your flyness, conquer your shyness"

-Kanye West

require lots of practice. Practice often consumes materials, not just time and effort, so be aware of this when deciding what to DIY and what to leave to the experts. That said, DIY often makes certain pieces more sentimental, so don't shy away from this if it's something you would like to do – and remember a beautiful thing is rarely perfect, so take a little pressure off yourself and enjoy the process!

Usually the florist who provides your bouquets, buttonholes and corsages will also provide any floral arrangements, so I won't rehash any of the information around choosing a florist. When it comes to décor you can go as minimalist as or as extravagant as you want (or can afford) when it comes to flowers. Examples of how floral arrangements can be included in the décor include:

- Columns
- Pew and row ends
- Arches
- Registrar's table
- Seating plan
- Table centre pieces
- The cake itself
- Photo frame or flower wall
- Floral letters

Do bear in mind though that floral arrangements can be expensive, and you certainly don't need all of the above. Though it can be tempting to adorn every surface with flowers, though maybe that's just me and my penchant for florals, less is often more. We had flowers for the registrar's table and table centre-pieces, and this looked simple but elegant – and we didn't have to re-mortgage the house to

Decoration

afford our flowers! Though maybe an arch or a flower wall would have been nice, I haven't lost any sleep over not having had enough flowers at our wedding.

My advice would be to get the most out of your floral arrangements by repurposing them throughout the day. For example, use the floral arrangement from your registrar's table on your top table, use your bouquet to sit alongside the cake at the reception, move any floral columns from the ceremony room to the reception venue and so on.

When choosing your décor, try to always bear in mind the overall picture and how it will all look together. We've all seen the toddler creating a card, covering it with 50 beautiful stickers and creating what some might call a busy mess. Remember, less can often be more – and your budget will thank you for this attitude too!

How To Plan A Wedding Without Killing Anyone

Summary

- Don't be afraid to stay true to yourself and your own unique style – even if you feel like you're copying Pinterest or a bridal magazine, only you as a couple will combine all of the elements in your own unique way – and this is beautiful!

- Pick a style and wedding colours you love and run with it.

- Be clear with the venue regarding what is involved in your package and what isn't.

- Make a plan of everything you want then be realistic as to what you will buy or find a supplier for, what friends and family will help with and what you will DIY.

- Always keep the overall look in mind, and remember less is often more!

Decoration

Decor ideas

Chapter Twenty-one

Flowers

Wedding flowers are a key detail of many weddings, they will likely feature heavily in the photos and make up a significant part of your wedding budget. For me, the cost of wedding flowers came as a big surprise! And not the good kind...

Flowers often feature in:

- Bridal bouquet
- Throwing bouquet (some brides choose to have a separate bouquet to throw)
- Bridesmaid bouquets
- Flower girl's bouquet, petals or pomander
- Corsages (typically worn by female relatives around their wrists)
- Buttonholes (typically worn by the groom, male members of the bridal party and male relatives)
- Hair crowns, bands or accessories
- Table centre-pieces
- Decorations, floral arrangements and archways

Flowers

- Aisle decorations

But the list is endless – you can decorate almost anything with flowers.

The downside of this can be the price. At our wedding we definitely compromised when we realised the cost of different floral arrangements. We also had a wonderfully savvy and helpful florist who suggested using the floral arrangements from the ceremony room to decorate the reception room and using my bouquet to lie alongside the cake for photos.

Where to start

If you're anything like me, flowers might be a rather intimidating part of wedding planning. I felt like I didn't have a clue what I wanted. I have no experience with flowers, other than the odd bouquets I've enjoyed being gifted. The issue is that when asked what I liked or didn't like about different bouquets, I wasn't really sure at all. I don't have a list of favourite flowers; I just know what makes me happy when I see and smell it. That said, you may be a flower expert – in which case my advice would be to draw up a list of the flowers you want and the colours you would like them in, then head to a couple of florists to get some quotes.

Assuming though that you're more like me: my advice would be to look through different flower guides online and also create a Pinterest board of flowers you like the look of. Once you have a general idea, I would advise creating a collage of pictures of flowers in styles and colours that catch your eye. I created three separate boards:

1. Bouquets
2. Buttonholes
3. Decorations and table centrepieces

These boards were simply A4 print outs of options I liked. If you feel a bit more confident you can have a look at what flowers are available during the season you are getting married in – though the florist should be more than happy to help with this.

I would then advise making appointments at three local florists based on reviews from family, friends, local bridal groups or websites. Take along the boards you have made and discuss them with the experts. Our florist was amazing – she looked at the boards and got my vision straight away. She was also able to tell me what wouldn't be possible – and suggest flowers that looked almost identical (to me) instead. She even talked me through which flowers

> **Top Tip**
>
> Don't be afraid to be honest with your florist about what you do and don't like – they need this information to understand your vision.

would be available but at a cost, and suggested alternatives to these too.

When choosing a florist, my advice is to go with your gut. Pick the florist who seems to understand you and your vision. Pick the florist who seems truly passionate about making your floral wedding dreams come true. Pick the florist that feels right to you. You likely won't have that much contact with your florist once you have agreed the plan until the big day, so it's vital to have someone you trust.

> **Top Tip**
>
> As with any vendor, don't be afraid to walk away if a florist doesn't seem to be understanding what you want – there are plenty more fish in the sea!

Artificial flowers

A different but increasingly popular option is artificial flowers – this can be, but isn't always, a cheaper option. Advantages of artificial flowers include:

- Less pressure on the timing of delivery as they don't wilt or die like real flowers
- No issues with allergies or hay fever
- They last forever – meaning you can keep them as a keepsake
- They aren't seasonal meaning you can have a wider range of flowers and colours

- They usually weigh a lot less

Though a lot of people are set on the beauty and smell of real flowers, these are pros definitely worth considering. Furthermore, artificial flowers have come a long way with some these days being of such good quality that it can be hard to tell they are artificial. My key advice here would be to invest in good quality artificial flowers though, as poor-quality ones can look very fake and be incredibly disappointing.

Preserving flowers

Following your big day, there are many options when it comes to choosing to preserve your flowers, if this is something that appeals to you. Though it can be expensive, I would recommend going for it as it's a once in a lifetime opportunity.

Most services ask you to send them your flowers as soon as possible following your big day (usually the day or two after – an ideal job for you maid of honour or best man). They then take a couple of months to dry and then preserve your flowers before sending the finished product back to you.

When it comes to choosing how to preserve your flowers, it's a very personal choice. Take a look on Pinterest for ideas, some include:

- Jewellery

- Resin letters or shapes
- Paperweights
- 3D box frames
- In a vase, decorative jar or presentation box

The possibilities are endless. For the more creative among us, you could even try to preserve your own flowers. Though I wouldn't recommend taking any risks here and definitely not trying it for the first time on your precious wedding bouquet – perhaps practice on a few shop-bought bouquets first, to make sure you are confident, if you choose to do it yourself.

These items can make very meaningful gifts for more sentimental family members and members of your wedding party. Friends of mine gifted earrings and necklaces made from their wedding bouquets to both of their mothers – who absolutely loved them. Such a priceless gift!

"A flower blossoms for its own joy"

-Oscar Wilde

DIY flowers

Some brides choose to either sort the flowers themselves or have a close friend or family member do so. This can be a great cost-saving option and also a wonderful way to personalise your wedding. Wholesale flower markets can be a good place to buy flowers in bulk.

> **Top Tip**
>
> Buy a few sample flowers first if ordering online in order to check the quality, rather than placing your whole order and then regretting doing so.

My advice here would be to take a class in flower arranging, or have your friend or family member do so, in flower arranging and practice before the big day. This can be a lot of pressure for a first-time flower arranger so don't set the standards unrealistically high with little practice. That said, with the appropriate amount of practice, patience and effort this can be a truly beautiful way to do the flowers for your wedding. I've been to several friends' weddings now who have done just this and they have all looked spectacular in their own way.

Confetti

In terms of confetti, most venues will only allow bio-degradable confetti. Some venues even ban confetti and insist on options such as bubbles or even sparklers instead. A good option for bio-degradable confetti is dried flower petals. This has the added benefit of smelling amazing!

Traditionally guests would bring their own confetti, but standard practice is now for the couple to provide confetti for guests, which is handed out by either bridesmaids or ushers as the guests line up ready to welcome the new couple. If you want guests to bring their own, then make sure to specify this on your wedding invites.

> **Top Tip**
>
> Don't go overboard with confetti – there are several confetti calculators available online that will indicate how much confetti you need based on the number of guests in attendance.

I would recommend looking online for confetti suppliers and picking a smaller, lighter petal that will fall slowly to the ground and so look better in photos. Typically, the confetti petals are similar to that of the rest of the wedding flowers – though there is no rule saying this must be the case. If there's a specific colour you would like which is only available in larger petals, add this to create a mix – this will look equally beautiful in the photos.

Flowers

You can also make your own confetti – whether this is by drying flowers, or hole punching leaves both are biodegradable so suitable for most venues. Two of my closest friends spent the year before their wedding collecting flowers from meaningful events and occasions (including my wedding!), drying them and using the petals to create their own confetti. I thought this was such a nice touch – and on their big day the confetti felt extra special and filled with love.

I would also recommend checking out Pinterest for creative ways to display and hand out your confetti to guests. There are so many options and this is a great way to personalise your wedding. From confetti cones, to trays of beautiful petals or even cute little sachets – the confetti display can itself be a beautiful decoration.

How To Plan A Wedding Without Killing Anyone

Summary

- Flowers are a key detail of most weddings and as such often make up a large portion of the wedding budget.

- Create boards of flowers you like – being aware of both the type of flower and the colour. This will make it easier to communicate your vision to the florist.

- Listen to your gut when selecting your florist – pick one who seems to understand you and communicates well.

- Artificial flowers and DIY flowers are becoming increasingly popular options and are definitely worth considering.

- Couples these days typically provide the confetti, which is often flower petals.

Flowers list

- Bridal bouquet
- Throwing bouquet
- Maid of honour and bridesmaid bouquets
- Flower girl
- Corsages
  - Mother of the bride
  - Mother of the groom
- Buttonholes
  - Groom
  - Best man and groomsmen
  - Ring bearer
  - Father of the bride
  - Father of the groom
- Hair accessories
  - Bride
  - Bridesmaid(s)
  - Flower girl(s)
- Table centre-pieces
- Decorations

Chapter Twenty-two

Music and Entertainment

When guests are questioned about their experience of attending weddings and what they remember most clearly, food and entertainment repeatedly top the lists. Though ultimately your experience of the day as a couple is what matters most, everyone wants their guests to have a great time creating lots of happy memories. On top of this, happy guests foster an uplifting and joyful atmosphere making the day more special and memorable (for the right reasons) for all involved. It is therefore essential to choose a good range of entertainment to keep your guests amused throughout the day and into the evening, especially at times you might be otherwise

> **Top Tip**
>
> If you do choose to have a playlist, leave a trusted friend in charge of it on the day, so you aren't fiddling around with it.

Music and Entertainment

occupied – for example during your portrait session, should you choose to have one.

Almost every wedding reception will have music at some point. Your first major decision here is whether you want a live band, a DJ or to create your own playlist and play it on some large speakers. This decision will be based both on budget and what you prefer as a couple, and any couples will choose to have a combination of the three. For example, you could have a live band playing with two or three sets and a DJ or playlist playing in-between these sets. Guests won't really mind whether you have a local band or a homemade Spotify playlist – as long as there is music playing that they recognise and feel comfortable dancing to, so don't feel pressure to splash out on an expensive live band if it's not something that's important to you. That said, if you love live music or have a band in mind that would make your evening, then go for it!

> **Top Tip**
>
> Make sure your speakers are appropriately sized for your venue and ensure there is somewhere to plug them in.

Once you've decided who and how you will play the music, it's a good idea to think about what songs you would like to be played. A band will usually discuss a set list with you beforehand and allow you to pick from a long list of songs they know. Most bands will be prepared to learn an extra song or two as a special request but will usually charge an additional fee for doing so. This is fair enough given the time they will have to put in to learning and rehearsing the new song(s) in order to perfect it ahead of your special day. DJs are often happy to be left to create their own playlists – if you hire a DJ you trust then this is ideal as they can read the room and play the appropriate song at the appropriate time using their professional expertise. That said, if you have specific songs or genres you want to be played or avoided then feel free to create a list for your DJ. Some couples include song requests for guests on their RSVP slips, so be sure to let the DJ know what songs have been requested if you have chosen to do this.

If you choose to create your own wedding playlist, do bear in mind that although you want songs that you love as a couple, you also want songs that your guests will enjoy (or even recognise if you have a more niche taste) and feel able to dance to. Try to pick a mix of songs along with the party classics – have a look online to find some wedding playlist classics if you are unsure what to include. Also remember that given your guest list will likely span several generations, it's nice to reflect this in your song choices too to make sure Mum and Dad aren't sat there wondering what on earth is going on. A good idea is to run the playlist by a couple of members of your family and the bridal party and take on board any useful suggestions they may have.

Once the music is sorted you can think about the rest of your entertainment. I would split this into two major categories: food and non-food. For simplicity we will cover each separately.

"People will never forget how you made them feel"
-Maya Angelou

How To Plan A Wedding Without Killing Anyone

Food

Food entertainment comes in the form of snacks, little extras or even an evening buffet or full meal option. If your guests haven't eaten since the wedding breakfast at 4 o'clock (sometimes even earlier) they will need sustenance in order to avoid hangry breakdowns and ensure they fully enjoy the evening. Evening guests (or those who weren't invited to the wedding breakfast) will also likely be expecting food.

Many reception venues will offer an evening buffet meal – this is an ideal option if you have a mix of guests who have recently had a generous wedding breakfast and guests who have just arrived, as each guest can help themselves to as little or as much as they would like. Make sure to discuss with your wedding venue what the options are and pick ones that will work well for you and your guests. It's a good idea to provide some seating too, as some people may much prefer to eat sitting down rather than standing and mingling. If your venue doesn't provide the option of an evening buffet, speak to them about bringing your own evening buffet caterer in to provide one instead.

In terms of snacks and little extras, the possibilities are endless! Pick options that reflect you as a couple and your guests will enjoy. For example, if your first date was at a pizza place then pizza might be a nice touch and a popular option. A few ideas to get your creative juices flowing, or just make you hungry, include:

Music and Entertainment

- Popcorn
- Cupcakes
- Churros
- Pretzels
- Ice cream
- Pic'n'mix sweets
- Cheeseboard
- Milk and cookies
- Hot chocolate
- Candyfloss
- Crisps and dips
- Chocolate fountain

Many of these options can be DIY'd or provided by a professional wedding vendor – choose what works for you in terms of time and money, but make sure not to overstretch yourself! A DIY bar for options like cocktails, hot chocolate or pimp your Prosecco always works well, as you can dress the table up to look quite spectacular. A fast food van is also a quirky option, though becoming more popular. Whatever you choose, make sure to run it by your reception venue in advance of booking, as some venues might not accept outside caterers or allow you to bring your own food in.

Entertainment

This is another great opportunity to personalise your wedding and to wow your guests, especially in the often-quieter periods where guests may be unsure what to do. Again, I would recommend thinking about what means something to you as a couple, that fits your budget and that your guests will enjoy. There are so many options, to name just a few:

- Magician
- Photobooth
- Wedding table games
- Party and lawn games
- Bouncy castle
- Caricaturist
- Guestbook
- Karaoke
- Space hoppers
- Mini-golf
- Sparklers
- Casino tables
- Palm reader

> **Top Tip**
>
> If there are children at your wedding, be sure to provide some age appropriate entertainment to keep them happy too - for example colouring books and crayons (these can even be personalised).

Don't be afraid to go more out-there and unique, especially with an option that means something to you as a couple. My husband is Bulgarian, so we hired a good-spirited and patient Horo teacher (a traditional Bulgarian dance performed at celebrations) to lead a 30-45-minute session teaching all our guests a few basic Horo dances. Though I'm sure most of us butchered the dance itself (myself definitely included, as I almost tripped over my husband's grandma!), our friends had a great time and often still mention it as one of their highlights. Our Bulgarian family loved it too! It really brought everyone together, and we had fun taking a few classes to find the right teacher beforehand too.

At an age when most of us are attending many weddings every year, it's nice to have something unique and exciting to set each wedding aside and make it more special, so don't be afraid to think outside the box. That said, the classics are always a hit too, so don't feel any pressure to go too crazy either.

How To Plan A Wedding Without Killing Anyone

Summary

- Entertainment is a massive part of the guest experience when it comes to weddings and can make your wedding stand out for all the right reasons!

- The first big decision is music – will you hire a band, a DJ or use a play-list, and what songs do you want played. Remember there is no right or wrong answer here – pick what works for you – every option can result in a great celebration when implemented well.

- Other entertainment can be separated into food-based and non-food based. It's a good idea to have snacks for your guests – after all a well-fed guest is a happy guest!

- The possibilities for entertainment are endless – don't be afraid to think outside the box and choose options that reflect you as a couple.

Entertainment

Music

....
....
....
....
....
....

Food-based

....
....
....
....
....
....

Miscellaneous

....
....
....
....
....
....

Chapter Twenty-three

Food and Drink

Wedding breakfast

Traditionally, following the ceremony, the newly married couple will sit down with their guests to enjoy their first meal together, referred to (rather confusingly in my opinion) as the wedding breakfast. This is often a sit down three-course meal, usually with either a set menu or options having been selected by guests with their RSVP.

Wedding breakfasts can be at unusual times, this is quite normal. What's important is to remember to keep your guests well-fed. If your wedding starts at midday but the wedding breakfast isn't until 4 o'clock then either warn guests in advance so they can prepare by treating themselves to a sizeable brunch, or provide canapés on arrival. A hangry guest is not a happy guest and whilst of

> **Top Tip**
>
> Include any menu choices in the invite to save having to go back to guests to ask them about menu choices later.

course the day is about celebrating you as a couple, hangry people do not celebrate well. In my opinion, the key here is good communication. As a guest, I find weddings where I don't know when I'm eating quite stressful, so at our wedding we sent out this information in advance. This might seem a little over the top, but our guests seemed to really enjoy being in the loop. Treat your guests as you would like to be treated and you can't go wrong!

In terms of food choices, my advice would be to select food that reflects you as a couple. If a sit-down meal doesn't, then choose something else such as:

- Buffet meal
- Sharing platters
- Pizza
- Ask your favourite local restaurant to cater
- Paella
- Hog roast
- Afternoon Tea
- Barbecue
- Crêpes
- Picnic

The possibilities are endless. A lot of couples overlook the wedding breakfast as an opportunity to individualise their wedding. It can also be a judgemental minefield in terms of more traditional guests who expect a sit-down three course meal. Don't let this put you off – pick a wedding breakfast that's right for you as a couple. Remember the best and most memorable weddings are the ones that celebrate you both, don't feel pressure to do what everyone else did!

Other food

Wedding celebrations usually go on well until the evening, so don't forget that guests will need further sustenance - especially if they last ate at 4pm!

An evening finger foods buffet can be an easy and crowd-pleasing solution to this, but this is also an ideal time to make tailored choices and pick what you like as a couple. Quirky extras often go down a treat with the guests - ideas include:

- Popcorn
- Sweets or pic'n'mix
- Doughnuts
- Cookies
- Cheese and biscuits
- Pretzels
- Candyfloss
- Pizza
- Bagels
- Tortilla chips and dips
- Cupcakes
- Smores

> **Top Tip**
>
> Ask your bridal party for ideas for this if you feel a bit stuck or overwhelmed. They will be happy to provide inspiration!

Food and Drink

This is again another opportunity to pick what you feel resonates most with you as a couple. Some couples even hire food vans, often a popular choice with guests. At a friend's wedding I tried Maltese Figolla for the first time – it was delicious! And it was so special as one of the bride's family was from Malta. Seemingly small but meaningful touches are what make weddings stand out, making them memorable for all the right reasons.

My suggestion here is to sit down as a couple and think about what food is meaningful to you both. What restaurants and cuisines do you both enjoy? Are there any foods that hold a special place in your relationships? Are there any foods special to your families or upbringing and cultures? If you're ever stuck – Pinterest is a great place for inspiration – though be prepared to get very hungry very quickly!

"Food is our common ground, a universal experience"

-James Beard

Food and Drink

Drink

Drinks are often considered an integral part of any celebration, for a wedding these include:

- Arrival or reception drinks (usually after the ceremony)
- Drinks with the wedding breakfast
- Toasting drinks
- Drinks throughout the evening reception

Traditionally there are one or two choices of arrival drinks, wine (usually a choice of a red and a white) is served with the meal and sparkling drinks (usually Prosecco or Champagne) are used for toasting. Typically, a bar will be available in the evening, if not throughout the day, serving other choices. If you enjoy your wine, this is an excellent opportunity to pick your favourites and share these with guests.

> **Top Tip**
>
> If you have no clue about wine and how to choose, ask a friend or family member who might know more. This is an easy way to get people involved in wedding planning in a productive and helpful manner.

An often-contentious topic across bridal forums is whether or not the couple should provide an open bar. This tends to be a very cultural thing. Americans typically see it as bad form not to provide an open bar whereas a cash-bar (where guests pay for what they drink) is more acceptable in the UK. I would argue this is a budgetary thing too. If you can afford it and want to, then offer an open bar. If you can't or don't want to then don't. Just remember that this is your day, and you will never please everyone, whatever you choose.

An increasingly popular option is to offer couple's cocktails – where the bride and groom each create a signature cocktail. This is an excellent opportunity to showcase your own tastes and wow your guests.

It's also worth remembering drink options can be alcoholic or non-alcoholic. My husband is tee-total and he very much enjoyed copious amounts of the "grown-up soft drink" at our wedding.

Food and Drink

Summary

- The wedding breakfast is your first meal together as a couple.

- This is traditionally a three-course sit-down dinner, but can be whatever you want it to be.

- Food and drink are an excellent opportunity to put your own unique spin on your wedding day – don't be afraid to showcase your food passions!

- Remember to provide enough food for your guests and tell them in advance when they will be eating throughout the day.

Food Ideas

Wedding Breakfast

Starter(s)...
....
....

Mains(s)...
....
....

Dessert(s)..
....
....

Other Food Ideas

....
....
....
....
....
....
....
....

Food and Drink

Drink Ideas

<u>Drinks</u>
Arrival……………………………………………………………………..
………………………………………………………………………………..
………………………………………………………………………………..
Dinner……………………………………………………………………..
………………………………………………………………………………..
……………………………………………………………………………….
Toasting…………………………………………………………………….
………………………………………………………………………………..
………………………..

<u>Other Drink ideas</u>
………………………………………………………………………………..
………………………………………………………………………………..
………………………………………………………………………………..
………………………………………………………………………………..
………………………………………………………………………………..
………………………………………………………………………………..
………………………………………………………………………………..
………………………………………………………………………………..

Chapter Twenty-four

The Seating Plan

Making a seating plan is often a notorious, even dreaded, part of wedding planning. In fact, some couples are even choosing to forgo a seating plan on the basis that adults are quite capable of organising themselves. The obvious advantages of this include, not having to create a seating plan (less work) and that guests can choose who they sit next to.

However, the disadvantages include people, especially those who don't know many others, finding it awkward to find a seat and larger groups finding it awkward to try and sit together. This can lead to scrambling and confusion when it is time to sit down. Furthermore, a seating plan can be fun to create and is an extra chance to show off your creative flair.

It's completely up to you if you want to do a seating plan or not. For the purpose of this chapter, we will assume you are doing one – if not, feel free to skip ahead.

The Seating Plan

Key considerations

The first consideration when making a seating plan will be your venue – the size and shape of the tables and where they are located. Your venue may be able to provide a plan of the tables to make envisioning who will be sat where easier for you.

The second thing to consider is the top table. This can be a tricky decision for more complicated families, and even when parents make assumptions they will be sat there. Pick what works for you – and always feel free to blame the venue if you feel awkward justifying your choice. There are several traditional options for this:

> **Top Tip**
>
> Ask the venue the maximum number for the top table – this can be a limiting factor but also an easy excuse if needed.

- Long traditional top table
    - Maid of honour or chief bridesmaid
    - Groom's father
    - Bride's mother
    - Groom
    - Bride
    - Bride's father
    - Groom's mother
    - Best man

- Alternative top table
    - Groom's mother
    - Bride's father
    - Maid of honour or chief bridesmaid
    - Groom
    - Bride
    - Best man
    - Bride's mother
    - Groom's father

- Sweetheart table – just the bride and groom

Don't be restricted by these options, choose what is right for you. Traditions seem to focus mixing the families in a boy/girl format. While this may work for some, it definitely won't for everyone! Families can be complicated – there can be friction between families, parents can be divorced and remarried, for example. In these situations, it doesn't make sense to exacerbate things by sitting people who don't get along next to one another, right in front of all your other guests.

We choose to have my husband and I with my parents on my side, and his parents on his side. Not traditional at all, but both sets of parents are quite reserved so we wanted them to be together. I also wanted the maid of honour and best man to be sat with their friends and partners rather than the top table – I felt they would enjoy this more. If you're

The Seating Plan

unsure about what to do, speak to people. It can be a nice touch to ask parents what they would like, if you don't mind or are confused what best to do.

Many people then choose to have family tables near the top table, it's up to you whether to mix the families or keep them on separate tables. This is a very individual decision, consider how the families will be more comfortable. After all, you will be looking out at these tables and it's more pleasurable to see a sea of happy, conversing people than a sea of awkward and uncomfortable looking people sat in silence.

A big decision for every seating plan is whether or not to mix the guests i.e. whether to sit people with those they know, or mix it up with the intention of guests getting to know each other. The latter can be an unpopular choice with guests. They want to enjoy themselves and being seated with someone they have nothing in common with can make for a painful few hours. Often weddings can be big reunions, a chance for people to catch up with friends in a happy and loving atmosphere. This means guests are often happier sat with people they know. Though it is of course your choice, and only you know how your friends and family will feel.

> **Top Tip**
>
> Sit people where you feel (or even ask) they will be most comfortable. A seating plan can feel like a lot of pressure but it doesn't need to be.

How To Plan A Wedding Without Killing Anyone

A singles table is also always a bad idea in my opinion. Whilst there's no harm in sitting two single friends you think might get along on a table together, don't make it awkward and obvious with a singles table. They will enjoy the day more sat with their own family and friends and will have plenty of opportunities to meet new people at other points throughout the day.

For weddings with lots of children, some couples choose to have a children's table. It's important to consider the age of the children here and whether it is appropriate for them to sit away from their parents, but it can be a good opportunity to get the children mixing on a table designed for them with activities and such to keep them entertained. Activities such as wedding colouring packs, and personalised colour-in wedding table cloths are great to keep children busy and ensure they enjoy the day too.

The Seating Plan

> "Someone is sitting in the shade today because someone planted a seed a long time ago"
> -Warren Buffet

How To Plan A Wedding Without Killing Anyone

Creating the seating plan

Okay, we have covered the seating plan basics, so let's get down to business to create the seating plan with an easy step-by-step guide:

1. Decide on the top table

2. Categorise all of the other guests, for example
   - Bride's family
   - Groom's family
   - Bride's school friends
   - Groom's school friends
   - Bride's college friends
   - Groom's college friends
   - Bride's university friends
   - Groom's university friends
   - Bride's work friends (different categories for different jobs)
   - Groom's work friends (different categories for different jobs)
   - Parents' guests

3. Count the number of guests in each category – there may be some natural full tables at this point, for

> **Top Tip**
>
> Print out or draw an A3 size table layout then write each guests name on a sticky tab. Position the guest's name on the table layout and move them around until you are happy. Then take a photo of this layout.

The Seating Plan

example if your tables sit eight and you have eight "bride's school friends" – this is a table sorted

4. Pair together groups that may mix well, chopping categories to meet table numbers. Whilst it is ok to split a category of friends, try not to leave one friend from a group alone. For example, pair four "bride's college friends" with four "groom's college friends"

5. If you have any lone friends (i.e. those attending who don't know anyone else) – use your knowledge around their interests to sit them with someone they'll get along with, ideally someone confident and chatty

Communicating the seating plan

There are a great deal of options you can use to create a seating chart to communicate the seating plan to your guests. Pinterest is definitely worth a look here for inspiration – there are some stunning uses of frames and mirrors, for example. This is a great opportunity for some DIY, if you want to showcase your creative flair. Equally there are many willing suppliers that make beautiful seating plans, guaranteed to impress your guests and look fabulous in wedding photos.

Typically, venues use numbers to refer to different tables, and this is an easy option to go along with. This can cause awkwardness though if some people (often family members) are displeased over who is sat on table number 2 vs table number 3. An easy way around this, and an opportunity to personalise your wedding further, is to name the tables. Tables can be named anything, though it's a nice touch to name them along a theme that is meaningful to you as a couple for example, meaningful places, flowers, films, songs, TV shows, and favourite characters. The possibilities are endless!

On the day, groomsmen and ushers are ideal to help people to their seats for the wedding breakfast. Individual place cards, though not essential, can help with this too, and are a nice souvenir for more sentimental guests.

The Seating Plan

<u>Summary</u>

- Seating plans are of course optional – but aren't as challenging to do as they may seem initially.

- Key considerations include:
    - The venue – size and shape of tables
    - The top table
    - Family tables – and whether to mix these
    - Deciding whether or not to mix the guests

- Creating a seating plan can be easier with a simple step-by-step guide.

- On the day, communicate the seating plan using a seating chart, some helpful groomsmen and ushers and individual place cards.

How To Plan A Wedding Without Killing Anyone

Seating Plan

Please note this is just an example, a layout from your venue will be much more appropriate.

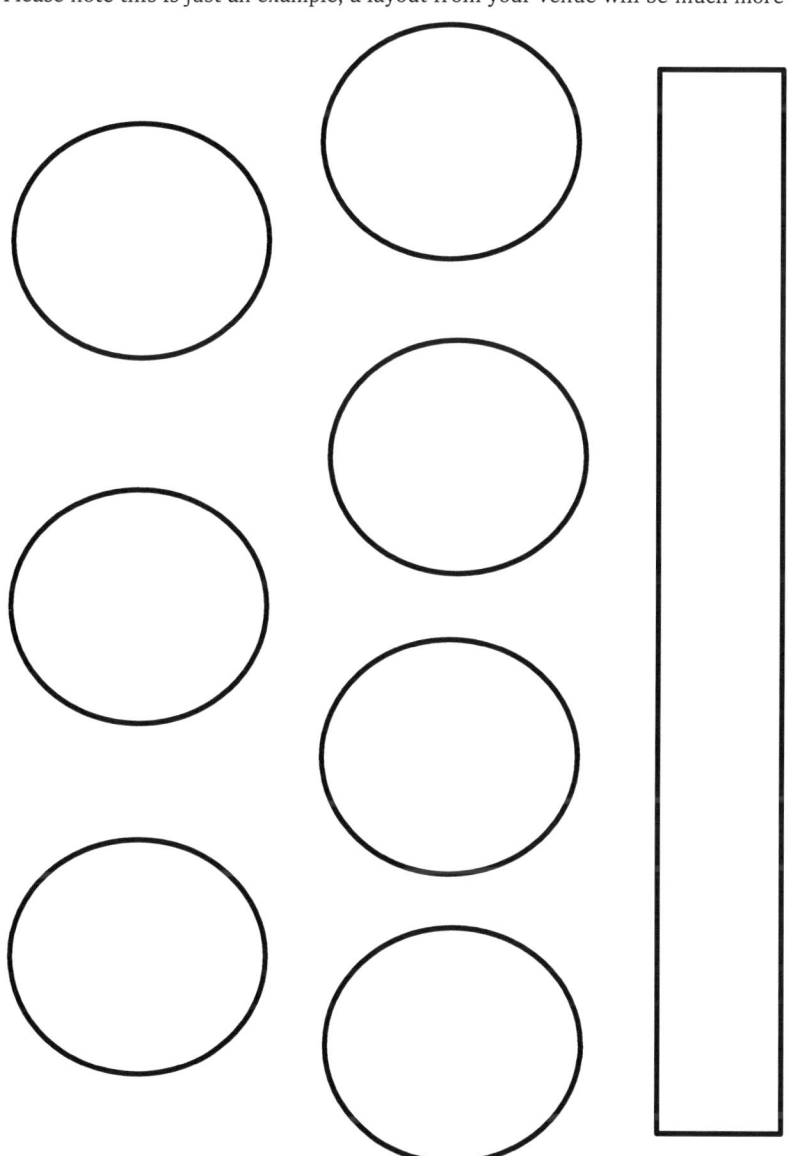

Chapter Twenty-five

Speeches

Speeches are traditionally given at the wedding breakfast, following dessert. As with everything though, this is your day and it's up to you when they take place. Some couples choose to do the speeches before the wedding breakfast; this is ideal if the speech givers are especially nervous as it allows them to get their speech out of the way and fully relax and enjoy the dinner. Others choose to do a different speech following each course – a clever way to overcome the potential speech fatigue guests may experience with several long speeches on the trot. There are no hard and fast rules, pick a time for the speeches that suits you best. Perhaps even discuss this with the people giving speeches and see if they have preferences.

> Top Tip
>
> Don't have too many people making speeches, this can get dull and repetitive. As a rule of thumb 3-5 speeches is more than enough.

In terms of who gives speeches, traditionally this is in the following order:

- Father of the bride
- Groom
- Best man

Don't be limited by these traditions, if it's not what you want. It is becoming increasingly popular for brides to make a speech too, and even the maid of honour or chief bridesmaid.

Typically, the father of the bride, or whoever makes the first speech will:

- Thank everyone for attending
- Thank those who contributed to the wedding
- Compliment the bride and recount a heart-warming tale about how special she is
- Welcome the groom to the family, and perhaps the rest of his family too
- End with a toast to the bride and groom

The groom will then usually open by thanking the father of the bride for his speech and toast. He will also:

- Thank the guests for coming
- Thank both sets of parents
- Compliment his bride
- Compliment and thank the bridesmaids
- Thank his best man and groomsmen

Speeches

- End on a toast

The Bride can then open by complimenting her new husband's speech and thanking the guests for sharing such a special day - you can see why this can end up a bit monotonous. The best speeches are from the heart, their meaningfulness making them unique. At a friend's wedding, the bride's mother and the bride both gave speeches, they talked about how the bride had overcome an eating disorder to grow into the wonderful woman she is today and to find the love of her life. These speeches honestly still make me well up remembering them!

The Bride will also typically:
- Thank her parents
- Thank the groom's parents and family
- Thank her maid of honour and bridesmaids
- Compliment the groom
- End on a toast

If the maid of honour or chief bridesmaid is giving a speech, she will typically:
- Compliment the previous speech-giver
- Thank the bride
- Thank the other bridesmaids

> **Top Tip**
>
> Only give a speech if you actually want to do so. I felt like I wanted to in order to balance the gender imbalance but on the day was so incredibly nervous – I hate talking to crowds! Do what you actually want to do.

> "Eloquent speech is not from lip to ear, but rather from heart to heart"
>
> -William Jennings Bryan

- Thank the groom
- Compliment the groomsmen
- End on a toast

The best man usually gives his speech last, as it is traditionally a more laid-back and jovial speech to end on, in contrast to the more sentimental ones that precede it. The best man will traditionally:
- Compliment the previous speech-giver
- Thank the groom
- Compliment the newlyweds
- Read any messages from absent friends and relatives
- Recount a funny (but not too risqué) tale or two about the groom
- End with a final toast to the bride and groom

These tips on what to include are very much just for guidance. It would be incredibly boring if every set of speeches at every wedding followed the same exact formula, but it can be a handy starting point. I remember not having a clue where to start and spending a lot of time on online trying to get a consensus. That is all this is intended as, a general guide around tradition to serve as a springboard for you to then pick what works for you.

At the end of the day, do what feels right. And remember, your wedding guests are people who love and support you and want this to be an incredibly happy and special day for you. My dad was incredibly embarrassed after choking up and becoming emotional during his speech. He paused for a few seconds, regained his composure and continued. Afterwards he was really frustrated this had happened, but talking to my friends they all found this incredibly moving with a few even saying this pushed them over the edge to tears. I myself even started crying at that moment. Your speeches will be perfect because they are given by the people you love, so don't feel under too much pressure in this area – though I (as someone who gave a speech) appreciate this is definitely easier said than done!

Speeches

Summary

- Speeches are traditionally given at the wedding breakfast following dessert, but can be given whenever you feel they fit best.

- Traditionally the father of the bride, the groom and best man give speeches, but speeches by the bride and the maid of honour are becoming more common.

- Despite these traditions, there are no hard and fast rules for speeches.

- Tailor the speeches, who gives them and their content, to make the day more personalised and unique and the guests will enjoy this part of the wedding a lot more!

Speeches

1st speech
Speaker………………………………………Asked……
………………………………………………………..
………………………………………………………..

2nd speech
Speaker………………………………………Asked……
………………………………………………………..
………………………………………………………..

3rd speech
Speaker………………………………………Asked……
………………………………………………………..
………………………………………………………..

4th speech
Speaker………………………………………Asked……
………………………………………………………..
………………………………………………………..

5th speech
Speaker………………………………………Asked……
………………………………………………………..
………………………………………………………..

Chapter Twenty-six

The Cake

Choosing your wedding cake is definitely one of the most enjoyable parts of wedding planning (who doesn't love a nice cake tasting!), but it can also be one of the more surprisingly expensive and hard to navigate parts. In this chapter we will break the process down into a series of more simple steps and decisions, to make it hopefully more straightforward and therefore more enjoyable.

Size of the cake

When choosing a cake, I would suggest it's best to wait until you've finalised and agreed upon a guestlist. You don't want to be short of cake, with people moaning they "never got a slice", but equally, unless you have a very large freezer, you don't want to be left over with lots of cake only for it to go to waste (especially given what you will more than likely have paid for the cake!). There are many guides that suggest slightly different amounts of cake per person but a rough guide, for a round cake (other shapes are of course an option too), is as follows:

Tier size in inches (cm)	Servings
5 (10)	8
6 (15)	12
7 (17)	18
8 (20)	24
9 (22)	32
10 (25)	38
11 (27)	48
12 (30)	56
14 (35)	78
16 (40)	100

The Cake

Bear in mind that some guests, and even yourselves, may take more than one slice - so do have some extra! A slice of cake alone in the honeymoon suite as a midnight feast is usually a dream come true.

Style of cake

When you've decided how many cake servings you need, play around with different numbers and sizes of tiers to see what works for you. Look online to see examples of different tier size combinations and to see what works visually for you.

In terms of what you want the cake to look like design-wise, I would suggest setting aside a bit of time to look online – Pinterest is always great for this! Create a board of cake styles you like. If you like, you can even sketch your dream cake. Don't be held back by any lack of artistic ability – you're not competing in an art competition, just trying to communicate your dream cake.

> **Top Tip**
>
> Decide on your overall wedding them and style before choosing your cake style, to ensure it is in keeping with your overall vision.

It's a good idea to consider and even choose what style of cake topper you would like at the same time as designing your cake, to ensure it is in keeping with the style of the cake itself. The possibilities are endless with cake toppers –

ranging from a simple Mr and Mrs lettering or figure to personalised lettering or even personalised figurines. Make sure to check out Pinterest and Etsy to see what is available. For an extra personal touch, my now husband and I actually made our own from Fimo modelling clay (other brands are available) – this probably wasn't the most impressive or professional cake topper ever used, but we had such a great time doing so and the guests loved it (or so they told us!).

> **Top Tip**
>
> Consider the weather when choosing your cake – certain icing or frosting may fair better or worse in warmer temperatures.

Meet with cake makers

Once you have an idea of the size and style of the cake, you are ready to speak to cake makers. My advice would be to look online and seek local referrals – find someone with a number of good reviews. Always look at photos of their previous work too. The wedding cake isn't a place to be saving money by taking risks, as a bad cake will put a real dampener on the day.

Call different cake makers, explain to them what you are looking for and get a rough idea of price. Follow your gut, arrange to meet up with a few who you feel comfortable speaking to and get a good feeling from.

"Romance is the icing, but love is the cake"

-unknown

Cake tasting

The best bit of choosing a wedding cake, and some might argue of wedding planning, is cake tasting. It's a good idea to bring along one or two wedding party members with you and your partner, just to get a wide range of opinions. That said, don't take the mick and invite the whole wedding party.

Some people prefer traditional fruit cake for a wedding cake, others plain sponge, but there are a wide variety of flavours on offer. My recommendation would be to try as many flavours as possible – even ones you aren't sure about as, like with the dress, you might be surprised by what you like. I've never been a massive fan of chocolate cake (shocking, I know!) but our cake maker's chocolate fudge cake was something else – so I was persuaded to have a layer of this in our cake.

When meeting with the cake maker, it's a good opportunity to discuss your design too – show them your sketches and ask them how feasible they feel it is. They may have suggestions too – hear them out as they are the experts after all and may suggest something you love.

Always discuss cake delivery and costs too – having the cake maker deliver the cake takes a great deal of stress off your plate on the day. They will have the appropriate equipment to safely transport the cake and the skill to save any little accidents, should they happen on the way. They will usually

The Cake

set up the cake for you too and often offer cake stands and ornamental knifes for hire.

After meeting with a couple of cake makers, decide which one you feel is best to go with – weighing up the tasting, the price, their reviews and previous creations and most importantly your intuition. Once you've decided, let the cake maker know as soon as possible and pay any required deposit to secure your date.

> ### Top Tip
>
> Beware family and friends offering to make the cake for you, often their heart is in the right place, but unless they know what they are doing (and you have seen their finished creations before) then it might be best to politely decline to avoid any awkward situations or cake disasters.

Other options

For those who don't want a wedding cake, there are many other options – from cupcakes or cake pops to cheese wheels, choose something that works for you. The message of creating a wedding that reflects and celebrates you as a couple has been repeated throughout this book, and that doesn't stop with a wedding cake. Another option is a dessert table (my sweet tooth is obviously influencing my suggestions here) – always a hit with guests! The possibilities are endless.

If you are looking to save money on the cake, department stores - such as Marks and Spencer - and some supermarkets have beautiful and often more affordable options. These are definitely worth checking out. It can be easy to get hung up on buying a massive expensive cake – but remember, when it comes to the cake, guests mostly only care that it tastes good, so don't place too much pressure on yourself thinking everyone expects a ten-tier masterpiece.

The Cake

<u>Summary</u>

- Once you know roughly how many guests are coming, use this to determine the size of the cake you will ideally order.

- Make some sketches to give the cake maker an idea of what you want from your cake and bring these along to any meetings.

- Don't forget to choose a cake topper, if you would like one.

- Choose a cake maker you feel comfortable working with.

- Always attend a cake tasting with your chosen baker, ideally a few different ones, before you order your cake.

- Remember to discuss delivery of the cake.

- If cake isn't your thing, don't feel you have to have a wedding cake. There are many different options, should you prefer.

How To Plan A Wedding Without Killing Anyone

The Cake

Chapter Twenty-seven

The Rehearsal Dinner

Wedding rehearsals are basically a practice of your wedding ceremony for you and your wedding party. These are particularly important for larger and more choreographed weddings with more complex arrangements. They give everyone involved a chance to practice their entrance and walk down the aisle, the order of events as well as where to stand or sit. Practice makes perfect and helps make sure everyone is on their a-game on the wedding day. It can also calm pre-wedding nerves and make everyone feel more confident that they know what they are doing on the day – yourselves included! The wedding rehearsal is usually followed by a celebration dinner for everyone involved, known as the rehearsal dinner.

That said, rehearsals are entirely optional and sometimes, especially for smaller weddings, can be unnecessary. Sometimes venues are not available prior to the wedding.

How To Plan A Wedding Without Killing Anyone

My venue wasn't available the night before, so I just verbally explained the key points:

- Order of entrances
- Where to walk
- Where to stop, stand, sit after they had entered
- Anything needed during the ceremony – for example when witnesses need to step forward

I set aside seating for the wedding party with decorative name tags and provided the order of the ceremony to wedding party members and immediate family in advance – so that they knew exactly what was happening and when.

Though the wedding rehearsal and wedding dinner are traditionally linked, you can still choose to hold a rehearsal dinner even without the wedding rehearsal itself. Or you can do neither – choose what works best for you and your guests given your situation.

> **Top Tip**
>
> If your venue is not available ahead of the wedding but you are keen for a rehearsal – one option is to rent out a room, tape out the layout and hold the rehearsal there instead.

The Rehearsal Dinner

When to hold the rehearsal

Traditionally the wedding rehearsal and dinner is held a day or two before the wedding itself. The advantage of doing it two days before, is that this gives you time to celebrate late into the evening (should you want to) as you have the following day to rest and recuperate before the big day. However, some guests may not be available or even have arrived for the wedding at this time, so do bear this in mind when planning the rehearsal. The evening before the wedding, by which time most guests have arrived, can also be an ideal time, as it can double as a welcome event for everyone and provide entertainment the evening before the wedding.

Who to invite to the rehearsal

Typically, the rehearsal includes yourselves, the officiant, immediate family and the bridal party. Sometimes guests who have travelled from afar may also be invited to the dinner afterwards. Given the idea is to ensure everyone knows what they are doing, anyone who has a role in the ceremony itself should ideally attend any rehearsals.

> **Top Tip**
>
> The dinner is a great time to distribute any gifts – smaller group means more time to hand out and open gifts.

"Practice creates confidence, confidence empowers you" -Simone Biles

The Rehearsal Dinner

The rehearsal dinner provides a nice, often more relaxed opportunity for family and friends to mix and mingle before the wedding.

Invites can be as formal or as casual as you like – some people choose to send off formal invites in their matching wedding stationery, others choose e-invites and others just let people know by word of mouth or a private Facebook event. There is no right or wrong way to do so.

What happens at the rehearsal

The wedding rehearsal usually involves a run-through of the wedding ceremony. It provides a good opportunity to practice entrances and walks down the aisle and who sits and stands where. Readings can be practiced, if you and the reader are happy to do so – though you may prefer to keep them as a surprise for the day itself. Similarly, vows will typically be kept for the day itself – but you could always say a few loving words to one another, should you wish.

Following the wedding rehearsal, the rehearsal dinner is usually held. This can be a formal sit-down meal, a meal at a local pub or backyard BBQ – whatever works best for you. Traditionally the groom's cake is served at the rehearsal dinner, but guests will

> **Top Tip**
>
> Use this gathering as an opportunity for any last-minute announcements of schedule changes or other important information.

likely be happy as long as there is food and drink. Some more formal dinners may have set menus, other dinners will have á la carte menus. Some venues may require guests to order in advance for larger groups

After everyone has eaten, there are usually some toasts. Often whoever is hosting the dinner (usually a polite way of saying paying for) starts the toasts. Traditionally the Bride's family would pay for and host the wedding day, and the Groom's family the rehearsal dinner – though this format is far less common in the modern day. This is also a good opportunity for anyone to give a speech who you wanted to but couldn't slot in on the big day.

> **Top Tip**
>
> Try not to stay up too late after the rehearsal dinner – you'll want a good night's sleep ahead of your big day.

Following toasts, there is usually time for a couple of wedding themed games to encourage people to mix and mingle and liven up the atmosphere. Popular games include:

- Mr and Mrs quizzes
- The shoe game
- Find the guest
- Advice for the newlyweds
- Bride or Groom

A quick google will reveal the rules of any games that you might not have heard of.

The Rehearsal Dinner

The key to a good wedding rehearsal and dinner is to relax and enjoy it - accept that things might not run exactly to plan, it is just a rehearsal after all! The rehearsal is a great opportunity to spend quality time with friends and family and to get the party started – embrace this.

How To Plan A Wedding Without Killing Anyone

Summary

- The wedding rehearsal is simply a practice run through of the wedding ceremony, to ensure everyone is confident of what's expected on them on the big day.

- This is usually followed by a special dinner to celebrate.

- Usually only the families and bridal party are invited – though again it's completely up to you – and rehearsals are held a day or two before the wedding.

- The rehearsal can be as formal or as relaxed as you want it to be, and some couples choose not to have one.

The Rehearsal Dinner

Rehearsal

Venue and location
....
....

Date
....
....

Rough plan
....
....
....
....

Invite list
....
....
....
....
....
....
....
....
....
....

Chapter Twenty-eight

On the Day Organisation

They say failing to prepare is preparing to fail, and while arguably, you can't fail at your wedding day (insert inappropriate joke here), you can still do your best to ensure it all runs smoothly on the day. You've spent months, potentially even years, planning your special day – so make sure to spend a little extra time planning your on the day organisation. But what exactly is meant by on the day organisation?

On the day organisation covers a whole host of tasks that will need doing on the day. For example, most couples will have personal decoration and little touches here and there that they have chosen to make their day more personal to them. Some venues will allow access the day or evening before, to allow you to set up but many won't. Given that you will likely be busy getting ready on the morning of the wedding along with your bridal party, it is essential that someone is assigned the task of setting up this personal décor. Whoever this is, it needs to be decided in advance and they need to be provided with a clear vision of how you want the venue to look.

The key to successful on the day organisation is delegation. Allocate jobs to people who you feel most confident in and can trust, based on the task. Tasks to allocate can range from who will meet the officiant and show them where they need to go to who will gather the different sets of guests needed for each different photo during the portrait session, if you to choose to have one. I've included a planning sheet at the end of the chapter covering a list of tasks and who will complete them. If this helps, complete this and add it to your organisation folder. Remember to allocate tasks appropriately based on people's skills – if time-keeping isn't someone's strongpoint, allocate them a less time-sensitive task.

If your budget allows then one option is to hire a wedding planner for the day of the wedding – often called a wedding coordinator. They will take on the task of ensuring everything runs to plan and sorting out any last-minute issues. This can mean one less worry for you on the day, making things less stressful and more enjoyable.

> **Top Tip**
>
> On the day of the wedding I would recommend leaving someone you trust in charge of the folder, the last thing you need to be doing on your wedding day is problem solving.

"Confidence comes from being prepared"

-John Wooden

On The Day Organisation

If you are going to invest in a wedding coordinator, my advice would be (as with any other wedding vendor) to ensure you check out their reviews (personal recommendations are even better!) and have met them beforehand to ensure you get on well and can fully trust them. The last thing you need is to pay out for a disorganised wedding planner who only adds to the stress! Wedding coordinators will usually start to get involved 4-6 weeks before the wedding in order to get fully on board ahead of the big day, but each coordinator's package will vary so be sure to discuss expectations of one another well ahead of time to ensure everyone is on the same page.

On the other hand, if your budget won't stretch to a wedding planner, you're just a bit of a control freak and want someone you know in charge, delegating tasks (or a bit of both, like me) then there is no issue with planning the on the day organisation yourself. Just be sure to get organised and plan in advance to minimise stress on the day.

> **Top Tip**
>
> Pick a folder that stands out but is in keeping with your wedding style, florals are always a good shout.

My biggest tip for organisation, and perhaps for wedding planning overall, would be to create a folder with all the key information in – with the first sheet being all your vendor's names (company and personal), their phone numbers, what they are expected to provide and when. I've provided an example table at the end of the chapter, but feel

277

free to adapt it however suits you best. In the folder I would recommend including:

- Hair stylist(s)
- Make-up artist(s)
- Photographer
- Videographer
- Transport company point of contact
- Florist
- Décor
- DJ and band
- Entertainment vendors

> **Top Tip**
>
> Note down other key information such as which vendors you are providing a meal for, who needs paying or tipping on the day.

Basically, just the details of every supplier that will be involved on the day.

I would always recommend having several copies of this folder – just in case one gets lost. Ensure that at least you and the groom have copies and potentially the maid of honour and the best man too.

This folder will almost certainly prove invaluable for "hiccup handling", as they call it in the business. A well-organised day with key information easily available to hand will mean that almost all hiccups can be handled, should they arise, before you're even aware of the potential issue.

Most venues will have a venue coordinator who will liase with you on the day regarding things you have directly agreed with the venue – these will vary greatly from venue to venue, so be clear what these are ahead of your special day. Don't confuse the venue coordinator for a wedding coordinator, they aren't there to solve non-venue related issues. If they do so they are going above and beyond!

My final tip for on the day organisation, and it's going to sound strange following several paragraphs detailing how to be organised, is to relax and have fun. Your wedding day will fly by, so don't waste time stressing the small things. You can't control everything, and something is bound to go wrong. When people told me this before my wedding this phrase would equally fill me with fear as to what might go wrong, and challenge me to ensure nothing did. On the day little things here and there inevitably "went wrong", but the truth is that I didn't even notice most of these on the day and I actually didn't care because the day was so amazing overall. So, relax and enjoy and remember all that really matters is that you get to marry and spend the rest of your life with your true love!

How To Plan A Wedding Without Killing Anyone

Summary

- Good preparation is essential to ensure the big day runs smoothly, don't fall at the final hurdle!

- You won't be able to handle it all yourself on the day itself – especially not if you intend to relax and enjoy your special day – so don't be afraid to delegate sensibly to people you trust.

- A wedding coordinator is a pricier option, but can really help with on the day organisation.

- Create a master folder with all the key information and contact numbers in – and have several copies of this folder!

On The Day Organisation

Wedding suppliers

What?	Who?	Email	Phone Number	Arrival
DJ	Dave	DJDave@hotmail.co.uk	01234 678 910	Sat Evening 6pm

Chapter Twenty-nine

Final Note

Once the wedding is all planned, though I assure you it will never feel perfectly planned and ready to go, I would thoroughly recommend taking a day off before the special day to relax and enjoy yourselves. A little self-celebration of all you've achieved – or a pat on the back, as they call it.

My final top-tip, so important that I've included it in the main text, would be to book a relaxing spa day for you and your partner the week before the wedding. On this day I would recommend wedding-chat is banned so the two of you can seize the chance to relax together. Wedding planning can be stressful and can cause tensions and arguments between you as a couple as well as between yourselves and family members. Take a day to let it all go and bask in your love for one another. Be sure to tell one other how excited you are to be marrying one another and talk about your future together. Let all the wedding planning stress go and embrace moving to an enjoyment mindset as you prepare to

Final Note

enjoy your special day. You've put so much time and effort into planning, now is the time to relax and enjoy. And remember, whatever happens on the day, the most important thing of all is that you are marrying the love of your life and will soon be wed – what happier thought is there than that!

Thank you for reading this book, I wish you and your partner the most magical of days and lives together. Remember that love conquers all – and that given you managed to plan a wedding together, you can do anything together… and may the love between the two of you continue to deepen and grow so much so that one day you look back at this period and your wedding day as the time you loved each other the least!

Acknowledgments

A big thank you to everyone involved in the creation of this book, especially my family. Todor, your hard work and determination has always been inspiring to me – my teammate and cheerleader, you continually help me to dream with my eyes open. Thank you.

Thank you also to my entire team, especially Gary and Grace. All experts in your own areas, who I am incredibly grateful and privileged to have worked with.

And to everyone else who has provided help and advice along the way. They say it takes a village to raise a child, this is also true when it comes to writing a book.

Printed in Great Britain
by Amazon